Of Love, Autonomy & Wealth:

Work and Play in the Virtual World (Your Guide to the

C-Suite)

By Patrick McCarty (award-winning author of *Archaeology of Mind*, *Rethinking*

Spirit, Host of *Insight Radio*)

and Baglan Nurhan Rhymes (SVP at AnchorFree)

I0483119

Includes interviews with:

·Raymond Ku, former CEO of McDonald's-Taiwan

·Carlin Flora, Editor with *Psychology Today* and Author of

Friendfluence

·Fran Hawthorne, Editor with *Fortune*, Author of *Ethical Chic:*

The Inside Story of the Companies We Think We Love

(named one of the Best Business Books of 2012 by Library

Journal)

"As celebrated economist Jeffrey D. Sacks has argued, there will be no return to prosperity in the absence of mindfulness, citizens who acquire the self-awareness to live as they ought. Patrick McCarty--award-winning author, 25-year university professor and radio personality--provides the means for the cultivation of mindfulness, a roadmap to joyous living, new horizons of possibility and financial prosperity. This is not your average self-help book. McCarty permits the reader to listen in on his conversations with a McDonald's CEO, an editor of Psychology Today, a writer for Fortune magazine, and other pioneers in contemporary thought. This book is a tour de force of erudition and psychological insight, all in the context of present-day globalization and techno-capitalism. This is a book to savor, to keep on hand always. It is a transformative reading experience, superbly written."

--CNN iReport

To Kelly, Brenden, Tyler, Emma, Bailey, Buddy and Twigs

"As celebrated economist Jeffrey D. Sacks has argued, there will be no return to prosperity in the absence of mindfulness, citizens who acquire the self-awareness to live as they ought. Patrick McCarty--award-winning author, 25-year university professor and radio personality--provides the means for the cultivation of mindfulness, a roadmap to joyous living, new horizons of possibility and financial prosperity. This is not your average self-help book. McCarty permits the reader to listen in on his conversations with a McDonald's CEO, an editor of Psychology Today, a writer for Fortune magazine, and other pioneers in contemporary thought. This book is a tour de force of erudition and psychological insight, all in the context of present-day globalization and techno-capitalism. This is a book to savor, to keep on hand always. It is a transformative reading experience, superbly written."

--CNN iReport

Foreword by Baglan Nurhan Rhymes,

Insight Communications' #1 Executive in USA

Aldous Huxley once said, "In an age of advanced technology, inefficiency is the sin against the Holy Ghost." There are abiding assumptions against which we can hardly be too vigilant. One is the assumption that Eric Schmidt, Google executive chairman, makes when he says, "Technology is not really about hardware and software any more. It's really about the mining and use of this enormous data to make the world a better place." This is the current and widespread assumption that the availability of "data" will work to achieve the transparency that opens societies up for the exercise of freedom that is democracy. It is one thing to ask whether this causal string of events ("data" causes transparency causes public discourse causes democratic institutions) is actually borne out historically. It is something else altogether to see that the terms involved are so duplicitous, taken separately or in relation to each other, that they constitute more of a problem for thought than a solution. And it is something else again to believe so wholeheartedly in the trinity of data, transparency, freedom that one speaks as a prophet, so certain of the inner mechanism of history, past and future, that to say otherwise is indeed a sin. Mark Zuckerberg, who parses Facebook's mission as to "make the world more open and connected," recently claimed, "We don't wake up in the morning with the primary goal of making money….There are a lot of really big issues for the world to get solved and, as a company, what we are trying to do is to build an infrastructure on top of which to solve some of these problems." Data mining and saving the world, the Internet as budding Valhalla, the tools that save humankind from itself—these are all elements in a utopian vision or regulative ideal that, I would argue, are harmful in their present form. I would argue that "data" is only as good as the interpretive mind that reads it, that can read it by seeing its significance in more than one context. I would argue that the Internet as a model for community—indeed, an ideal community without borders—is deeply flawed, that without borders there is no community at all. I would argue that the optimism borne of the belief that our tools or technological progress will save humankind is part of what most centrally ails humankind, and I say this not only because it is hard to imagine the window between the invention of the ballistic missile and the anti-ballistic missile closing. That is, for as long as this window obtains, so does the opportunity for disaster, the possibility that over time becomes a near certainty.

In the so-called "marketplace of ideas," the telos of all human progress is the elimination of inefficiencies, rather as Huxley had it. We must bear in mind, however, that these "inefficiencies" overlap considerably with the resistance that is reality. The regulative ideal guiding the online experience is the absence of inefficiencies, a frictionless surface in which nothing obstructs movement, and it is this same ideal that has become the single greatest force in the offline world. The telos to which all things today converge is the absolute obviation of resistance. Evgeny Morozov tries to envision the future from a Silicon Valley perspective. "If Silicon Valley had a designated futurist, her bright vision of the near future—say, around 2020 or so—would itself be easy to predict. It would go something like this: Humanity, equipped with powerful self-tracking devices, finally conquers obesity, insomnia, and global warming as everyone eats less, sleeps better, and emits more appropriately. The fallibility of human memory is conquered too, as the very same tracking devices record and store everything we do. Car keys, faces, factoids: we will never forget them again." Morozov goes on with his rather extended hypothetical. Technology will make the backroom deals of politics impossible. Political parties are replaced by the users who used to bowl alone coming together— exactly once—to vote, and disband forever more. The unimaginable wealth of data dries up the swamp pit of Washington lobbying and pay to play. Voters are pressured, gamed or otherwise incentivized to vote directly from their smartphone, saving them a trip in the self-driving car.

We must have the courage for a hermeneutical turn. We must be the first, as leaders in the field, to resist messianic fantasies. Such ideals exert the profoundest influence, narrowing the landscape of the imagination. While America has long been automobile-centric, it has always been possible to imagine things otherwise. Our faith in the Internet is such that we cannot imagine a world without it. We ought at minimum be agnostics in this far from scientific faith among cyber-intellectuals in the Internet for what we consider progress, the promotion of democratic sentiments and parliamentary government. We should not anticipate the dawn of a neoliberal paradise.

An assumption dating back to 1989 is that the democratic forces of the world had won and that all borders had been thrown open to techno-capitalist consumerism, the natural outcome of the lifting of barriers to trade. This has for so long been the operating assumption that it lies at the basis of much of what the IMF has done in the world for the last 50 years. Funds are extended in exchange for so-called free trade. And it was this assumption that made the Francis Fukuyama thesis on the end of history plausible. Starbucks, MTV, and Google were inherently liberating. What wasn't understood sufficiently was the degree to which we were seeing ourselves in the other. Just because North Korea wants to exist in a less than splendid isolation does not mean that authoritarian regimes cannot employ all the technologies we associate with the Internet toward their own ends. Authoritarianism today has been repackaged. Marx's Grundrisse is out, Apple electronics is in. Che Guevara is out, keeping up with the Kardashians (conspicuous consumption) is in. Much of the developing world has discovered that hedonistic consumerism looks pretty good, and they have taken to it much as Elizabethan Europeans once did to tobacco and native populations to fire water.

Concrete support for the case I am making can be found in the great expectations that attended the so-called color revolutions of the former Soviet Union. The true beneficiaries of them have been Russia, Azerbaijan, and Kazakhstan, terra incognita with respect to the end of history. Sports cars and pricey holidays, it turns out, coexist quite well with despotism. Surely we should never forget that the Roman citizen traded in the vote for bread and circuses. The wars in Iraq and Afghanistan have only given democracy promotion a bad name. The persistence of authoritarian regimes in Belarus, China, and Iran has nothing whatever to do with a Western failure of the will. If we have largely lost the courage to promote democracy in the world, it is perhaps the result of a fundamental misreading of history, a hermeneutically unsound approach.

It was a part of the conventional wisdom that the Soviet Union collapsed because of contraband photocopiers and fax machines, which then promoted samizdat. Radio Free Europe and the Voice of America had broken through, communicated to the world that toothpaste and toilet paper need not be precious commodities. Cold War triumphalism, after decades of funding more and more advanced munitions, left in its wake, in the absence of geopolitical bipolarity, the conviction that technology and modernization were deadly to repressive regimes. But this has to no small degree been an ideology in the service of existing power. Big global capital has never done better. The Internet has been anointed in oil, has taken on magical properties, and it is thought that its mere existence enables users to discover the horrors of the authoritarian homeland and the irresistible allure of democracy, that the sweet tweet of freedom is music in every ear. But the state is not the only form of oppression in the world today. We perhaps have not sufficiently digested this realization. We commonly speak of the president of the United States as not having the power one might think, but that isn't because we think Congress or the UN has it. It is because of "vested interests," the fact that Washington is awash in influence and up to its eyebrows in undertakings that have nothing to do with Main Street. It isn't just the 1% or Wall Street or the stock market that bears little resemblance to the average citizen. Technology has created a world in which nation-states are growing increasingly marginal. My argument is not that the neoliberal utopians overestimate the Internet. It is that they vastly underestimate it.

The Soviet Union, conventional wisdom once had it, was undermined by the dissemination of information, cheaply reproduced pamphlets. China, surely, it would seem to follow, cannot survive its own bloggers. The assumption invoked here now has a name. It is called the Google Doctrine, which has been defined as "the enthusiastic belief in the liberating power of technology accompanied by the irresistible urge to enlist Silicon Valley start-ups in the global fight for freedom." The notion is that somehow the Internet just naturally works to the advantage of the oppressed rather than their oppressors. But we know, upon rational reflection, that the Internet is not one thing, that it is an enormously complex and constantly evolving system that can be adapted quite well to propagandistic ends, to the surveillance needs of dictators, to sophisticated forms of censorship. The people, the great masses, it is thought, will rebel, cyber-mobilize and overthrow obnoxious regimes. My thesis, however, is that the Internet is more powerful than the technology romantics have it. It is that the Internet is powerful enough to reshape any kind of regime whatever, democratic or not. It is obviously a dangerous narcissistic fantasy to look out into the world singlemindedly preoccupied with the question, when will they become like me? When will they be propaganda-free, noble and free, free but responsible citizens. When will they find themselves free to be me?

And now we can see that this is the oldest endogenous theme in history, the unwillingness to permit the other to be other, to look long and hard enough into this otherness to become better democrats ourselves. One influential commentator has described his own experience in these terms: "I myself was intoxicated with cyber-utopianism until recently….My own story is fairly typical of idealistic young people who think they are onto something that could change the world. Having watched the deterioration of democratic freedoms in my native Belarus, I was drawn to a Western NGO that sought to promote democracy and media reform in the former Soviet bloc with the help of the Internet. Blogs, social networks, wikis: We had an arsenal of weapons that seemed far more potent than police batons, surveillance cameras, and handcuffs. Nevertheless, after I spent a few busy years circling the former Soviet region and meeting with activists and bloggers, I lost my enthusiasm. Not only were our strategies failing, but we also noticed a significant push back from the governments we sought to challenge. They were beginning to experiment with censorship, and some went so far as to start aggressively engaging with new media themselves, paying bloggers to spread propaganda and troll social networking sites looking for new information on those in the opposition. In the meantime, the Western obsession with the Internet and the monetary support it guaranteed created numerous hazards typical of such ambitious development projects. Quite predictably, many of the talented bloggers and new media entrepreneurs preferred to work for the extremely well-paid but largely ineffective Western-funded projects instead of trying to create more nimble, sustainable, and, above all, effective projects of their own. Thus, everything we did—with generous funding from Washington and Brussels—seemed to have produced the results that were the exact opposite of what my cyber-utopian self wanted."

We can't afford to be deaf to social, cultural, and political nuances and indeterminacies. It is all too easy to treat the Internet as a fait accompli certain to impose its irresistible logic everywhere. The Internet is by no means a finished thing and it is misleading to speak of it in the singular—for then it becomes too easy to think of it as one thing. Freedom will need to be protected against powerful companies like Google and Facebook. It just isn't clear that the Marxian materialist conception of history as technology-driven can be taken on faith, for that is our faith.

If we care to know something about the object out in the world, it might be helpful to take a closer look at ourselves. The so-called "Twitter Revolution" of Iran some years ago is perhaps the clearest illustration. We looked on this uprising and saw the power of technology, the mobilization of discontent via tweeting. In fact, this was so much the conventional wisdom that it became the prism through which we experienced subsequent events in Egypt. The truth, however, lies elsewhere. On the eve of the Twitter Revolution there were precisely 19,235 registered Twitter accounts in Iran. That is 0.027% of the population. Tweeting internal to Iran was hardly a factor at all. But we in the West look on, and like people everywhere, tend to see ourselves. We see our own deepest faith—the inexorable progress for the good of data dissemination and technologies of communication. This is a messianic view, a religious view. It is the messianic component of Marxism, which anticipated the withering away of the state. It is the messianic element in Hegel which gets parroted as the "end of history."

Inefficiency is not a sin against the Holy Ghost, as Malcolm Gladwell so powerfully demonstrated in his book David and Goliath. The absence of transparency, the resistance of opacity in the other, is the only opening we have to progress of a human kind. The resistance of the world to us is indispensable to the experience of being in the world, to having a purpose. Jeffrey Sacks, the IMF and Harvard economist, has written a surprising book in which he claims that there will be no real economic recovery until the people involved, the consumers, become mindful. Now there is a curious injunction for an economist. He even makes reference to Socrates and his famous dictum, "Know yourself." He dwells at some length of the subject of Buddha. So it would seem that my central contention here is not so radical after all. The key, it seems to me, to the most efficacious and responsible use of the Internet is a mindful one. Let our skepticism be healthy. And it can only be this if we put away our utopian ideals, for they all too readily become guiding stars.

The following book should prove useful to anyone, especially women, who seek the self-discovery, the clarity of purpose, requisite to life in the largely male-dominated C-suite. I have done numerous CNN radio shows with Patrick McCarty, and he is truly a host with as much heart as message. To hear our discussions, go to insighttalkradio.com. It has been a pleasure to serve as his technology advisor over the years.

In the pages below, I share the insights of the former CEO of McDonald's-Taiwan, Raymond Ku; of Carlin Flora of *Psychology Today*; and of Fran Hawthorne of *Fortune*, all of whom have been guests on my radio program. I consider the most advanced thinking on the subject of the reintegration of our personal and professional lives, the reclamation of our spiritual well-being and economic prosperity. My central question, for the guests on my radio program and in this book, is the same: How can one flourish both as a human being and as a working, productive member of society in our strange new world of hypermobile techno-capitalism?

This book does not promise to be an easy read. An easy read is not one that can change fundamentally your view of things. This book promises to be a radical deconstruction of and revolution in your foundational assumptions, in your experience of the world, both personal and professional. This book promises that if you will read it through, preferably more than once, you will emerge "someone else," a dramatic shift will have occurred in the quality of your experience, and that this shift will benefit you not only professionally and interpersonally, but in every way.

There is no need to worry whether these are empty promises. The shift I speak of won't come all at once, at the end of the book. It will occur while you are reading along. You will sense it at every turn. This book is at once didactic and performative. That is, its assimilation is transformative, and the transformation it induces facilitates even deeper assimilation.

If an author could simply secure you what you need in a set of declarations, pronouncements from on high Moses-style, everyone would be done with "it" by now and on their way to the stars. Every high-level Power Pointed business conference would be an *open sesame*. Yet statements in isolation are rarely if ever meaningful. People are in a hurry, having more and more taken on the metabolism of a jackrabbit, and they want easy answers. This book is both a response to these people and a challenge to our most fundamental assumptions.

The quest for easy answers is a trap. It creates an opportunity for fast-talking profiteers to make a buck and leaves the reader much as he or she was before. In the psychotherapeutic community, the notion of an "easy fix" is something of a contradiction in terms (though insurance companies demand them all the same). Instead the greatest thinkers in the field tend to speak of a "working through," and working, in this context, suggests a certain necessary effort, a willingness to persevere against certain obstacles, even uncomfortable ones. Given this, what would it mean if I offered a garden path, a *Dummy*'s guide, *Sparks Notes*? It would suggest a performative contradiction. My authorship of this book—this performance—would contradict the content of it, *how it is* colliding with *what it says*.

This book constitutes a test. If you can read it and truly take it to heart, you will have taken what Robert Frost called "the road less traveled," and it will indeed make all the difference. This book accomplishes two objectives simultaneously, one expressive and the other enactmental. It is expressive in the sense that concepts are presented that are perhaps new to you. It is enactmental in the sense that the book is itself an instantiation of the content. You will read and acquire a great many useful ideas, and the very process of reading will create within you new habits of thought and hence a fresh experience of the world, an invigorated awareness of possibility. But, first, a thought experiment.

Imagine the drawing on paper of a square situated inside a square that is larger and that utterly contains the smaller one. If while pondering the figure, I suggest that it is a tunnel, your experience easily accommodates the interpretation-guiding notion. The smaller square is de-substantialized as the empty space at the end of the tunnel and the intervening area between squares is substantialized and extended backward spatially as the receding walls of the tunnel. If instead, however, I suggest that the drawing is of an open-topped box, the smaller square is substantialized, set at a distance, and the larger square represents the open top, which is drawn nearer in the line of vision. If I suggest that the figure is the view from above an outward tapering lampshade, the smaller square is again de-substantialized and the area between the squares is extended away in space as the outer sides of the shade. Experience is always organized by thought, by the ideas we entertain. If you have a phobia of spiders—the set of thoughts that accompany fear in this respect, your experience of the creature will be wildly dissimilar from mine, for I might find them cute or quirky. Hallucination as a phenomenon is only possible because our thoughts are always already quite visible. The genius

Wittgenstein demonstrated this with his famous duck-rabbit drawing.

Ralph Waldo Emerson, the great American essayist, once recommended what he surely knew the overwhelming majority of his readers would resist: passing an entire day attending with singular focus to one's own thoughts. Emerson's view was that rarely has one preoccupied with cheerful thoughts ever succumbed to despair. Emerson could say this not because he was so hopelessly pre-Prozac, but because he recognized something that looks very much like truth. Our bodies are not our principal concern. No thought goes into digesting a sandwich. Our bodies do it for us, directing the nutrients to where they need to go. The body's operation is remarkably intelligent but, thinks Emerson, this is not the kind of intelligence that ought to concern us most. It is not the kind that makes us free, beings of opportunity, of choice and commitment.

If we are in fact free to choose, possessed of free will, this cannot reside in any simple fashion in our bodies. Our bodies seem to belong to the iron-clad necessity of cause and effect, the laws of biochemistry. As such, if there is an arena in which freedom is possible for us, it resides in our thoughts, our conscious experience. And, indeed, the idea of personal responsibility, even in the realm of jurisprudence, suggests very precisely conscious decision and the thought that goes into it. In other words, it suggests my control over the course of my thinking. Hence, we distinguish between those who have reached the age of reason and all others, the sane and the insane, the premeditated act and the unpremeditated.

My body must respond as it will to diet and exercise and genetics and environmental factors of all kinds, for it is determined through and through, or so the argument goes. The body belongs to nature, the realm of the physical sciences, of the laws of strict necessity. If there is in fact human freedom, Emerson believes, it can only have its rightful place in the province of the mind. We are free to think and to think differently, at any time to begin the process of acquiring new habits of thought that serve us better, what Aristotle included in his conception of a "second nature"; there is always the infinite promise that Kierkegaard always identified in "the moment." There is no privileged time for beginning to acquire the second nature that accompanies new habits of thought. Every moment is a moment of decision.

Our everyday experience has to be understood in terms of two rather distinct aspects of mind, the conscious and the subconscious. Consciousness can be thought of in terms of what is manifestly occupying your mind at this very moment (e.g. the words on this page). The subconscious bears a direct relationship to what has been thought and done. So, for instance, it is possible to drive the highway listening to the radio, consciously preoccupied with music, and come to the sudden realization that you don't remember the last twenty miles. In other words, your subconscious mind was attending to the mechanics of driving while your conscious mind was preoccupied with the radio, and no memory persists of the road, though you doubtless were alert to it. The fact that you stayed on the road proves it.

In that this distinction between conscious and subconscious is so critical, consider another example. Let's say that at present you are entertaining thoughts of eating healthy tonight. These thoughts, as you perhaps know from experience, will not necessarily prove decisive. Programmed into your subconscious mind might be the need for the stimulating toxins of processed foods. What will result? Almost certainly conflict. You will be torn between what the conscious mind knows to be best, the healthy option, and what the subconscious mind is used to getting and desires. Foods, whether natural or synthetic, are habit-forming and the subconscious comes to want only more of the same. The case of an addict is an extreme illustration. An addict may know that continued abuse will mean premature death, with perhaps madness and disgrace first, but the subconscious mind will perpetuate the destructive behavior regardless. Consciously the addict can be convinced of the need to forego the substance. But the subconscious in its insistence upon continued use brings the addict into conflict and, not atypically, to yielding to the temptation. What is to be done? How does one take hold of the moment?

In that the contents of the subconscious are created over time from consciousness, we can attend to transformation at the level of consciousness, change the way we think and perceive. We can acquire the discipline, through practice, of attending above all to our own thoughts. The subconscious is waiting to be created, to be cultivated in such a way as to serve you much better, and that means that you can begin right now, that you can make consciousness a focal point of your concerns and cultivate the experiences and habits that are in your best interest.

Conflict can be maximized (as it is for those who "love drama") or minimized. The first thing you will discover is this: The activity of consciousness, when it itself becomes the object of awareness (with self-consciousness), is dramatically altered. The raised consciousness of what we are thinking from moment to moment immediately transforms our thinking. And this is not only because we begin to see that we hold some misguided beliefs. It is also because only in this way, given the relationship between thought and freedom, can we experience genuine self-possession. We recognize the poise of self-possession in others, but it has to be solidified within ourselves for it to have meaning.

The subconscious mind is a vast archive that contains everything you have ever experienced. If you wish to prove its existence, simply call to mind the phenomenon of having something "on the tip of your tongue." You hear a song, know you know the title, but can't quite recall it. Perhaps, later, in the middle of some other activity, the title just comes to you. You did "know" it all along. It was in your subconscious. Moreover, your subconscious reads it off, identifies it as a content, communicates this knowledge to consciousness, but not the content itself. The failure of recollection was the failure to retrieve it from the subconscious archive so as to make it conscious. Needless to say, this archive can become so vast that its powers seem irresistible, and things in life predestined. Patterns emerge and repeat (in the choice of friends, spouses, occupations, and so on) and you feel yourself the plaything of forces at large, a victim of fate or circumstance. The subconscious would have us repeat, and then leave us wondering how we have come to do the same damn things over and over again.

If you grew up in poverty, your subconscious understanding will conform to what goes into poverty, what sustains it. And, as you know, it is possible to remain poor, materially speaking, for a lifetime—even across generations. Do those who remain sunk in poverty desire it? Do they enjoy being poor? Or are they involved in a kind of vicious repetition? It would perhaps be accurate to say that poverty is what they know and that some very persistent habits have formed on the subject of accumulating wealth (e.g. the means for doing it, the lifestyle or habits necessary for it, the frame of mind, etc.). It remains the case that those born into affluence are more likely to remain affluent, those born into poverty poor. It isn't that there are no exceptions, obviously, but this remains the general tendency. And this fact is no more surprising than that a woman from rural India who has just learned to drive an automobile after a lifetime of riding pack animals tries to listen to the radio while driving and ends up in a ditch. After all, she didn't even grow up with a rough working knowledge of cars and streets and traffic. She can eventually learn to "multitask" while driving, but it is unlikely to come as readily to her as to those in an automobile-centric society, those already immersed in that culture.

A very high percentage of people, even among those who have attended college and earned a degree, have little financial literacy. They don't know how money "works." The woman from the hinterlands of India, if she studies the rules of the road and practices, has an excellent chance over time of becoming as good a driver as anyone else. But without an initiation into the rules, the laws and principles that govern a given discipline, how is one to become proficient? Those without financial literacy cannot be expected to make good choices. They don't know the "rules of the game," the strict necessity of which is clear whether at what is at issue is playing the piano, speaking a language, moving pieces on a chessboard, or dropping back to throw a pass.

In this book, you will be initiated into a new understanding of health, wealth, spirituality, and vitality. That is, reading this book will start you upon the process of rewriting your subconscious mind so as to better serve you, both in the short and long term. At first, the steps involved will have to be grasped very thoroughly at the conscious level. This is not surprising at all. Were you to learn for the first time to dance or play the piano or type, would it be unusual for you to be consciously vigilant of the movement of your feet or hands? In fact, it is not uncommon for the beginner's dance steps to be quite literally painted on the floor. How better to establish their *conscious* significance?

The repetition of practice and rehearsal (e.g. memorization) can only be understood accordingly. It functions to secure the conscious foothold that prepares the way for subconscious mastery. And mastery is grace. Someday you will be able to type or dance or play the piano while you are thinking consciously about other things. You will enter the hall for the history examination having studied so thoroughly and well that you can clear your mind, for you no longer have to repeat what you have committed so successfully to memory. You certainly don't expend conscious effort to walk from your bed to the shower. It isn't as if, your mind being elsewhere, you regularly run smack into the bed and fall down. In fact, if I maliciously intended to destroy the masterful ease of a fellow pianist, what tactic would be better than to suggest to him or her what it might be like to be doomed to full conscious awareness of every finger movement? If I succeeded in implanting this idea, my competitor would be vanquished. The feeling of mastery that typically accompanies subconscious possession would abandon him or her. Indeed, when I have a "tip of the tongue" experience, what tells me that I possess the sought after information is not itself information or reasoning. It is a feeling, an intuition, a sense of certainty ("I just know that I know the title of that song, though I can't recall it.") The subconscious communes with feelings, moods, qualities of experience that are immensely intelligent.

There is also a thickening of consciousness that renders us stupid. The person who is shy in social situations might complain that her mind at these times goes blank and that she can't think of anything to say. What really happens is that the anxiety that attends painful self-awareness thickens consciousness, invokes it in too great a degree, and paralyzes her intellect. Surely the same phenomenon is what is at work in so-called test anxiety. The graceful subconscious is stymied.

The conscious mind is the seat of immediate perception, our window onto the world. However, this conscious experience is through and through shaped, organized, articulated by subconscious contents. If, for instance, I have grown up in the hinterlands of India, deep in the agricultural regions of draft animals and subsistence farming, I would not hear the rumbling of an automobile engine the way an urbanite would. In fact, on first encounter, I might find the racket quite unsettling and "ugly." Over time, however, the sound and what it means (the noise as the noise of the engine) become one and the same thing. The same is true, obviously, of a word in my native language. I don't hear the "noise" expelled from the lips and then chase it down for its meaning. I don't hear the noise and then realize shortly thereafter that the noise that has been uttered is actually the word "cat." Indeed, the acquisition of a foreign language is precisely the business of narrowing this gap. We are fluent when the gap has vanished.

The conscious mind is also given form emotionally. That is, it is driven by love, fear, hope, despair. Most people, for instance, fear death and much of their attention is devoted to warding it off, whether by eating, planning for the future, or embracing superstitions. But when push comes to shove, is the fear of death actually the fear of becoming nothing (at least with respect to bodily life) or of descending into a poor quality of life? If we were afraid of not being (of being nothing), one would think the period prior to birth as capable of inducing terror as the period after death. What of the couple that has been married for so long that the death of one leads to the death of the other? Ask the elderly what they fear most, and over and over again, study after study, it turns out not to be death, but loss of dignity, a poor quality of life. We often lose sight of the good, of that which remains valuable, of the standard of value by which all other priorities can be organized. And so we are vulnerable to wasted lives in pursuit of cotton-candy nothings—stimulation, cheap pleasures, diversions, distractions, amusements. When that which we identify as the good, either with reason or without, is taken from us, the result can literally be fatal. At the very least, there can be a debilitating loss of purpose. And purpose is all-important. This book is very largely about rekindling purpose, what purpose means, and how the quality of our daily experience grows out of it.

Perhaps the greatest danger to life is living it on automatic pilot. We need to periodically ask ourselves, quite consciously, as to the nature of the overriding objectives of our lives. As we change, so should our objectives. To continue in the pursuit of objectives that have lost their personal meaning is rather like jogging in a cul-de-sac, only it isn't nearly as healthy. Every moment is a moment of decision. It is always possible to decide. It is always possible to take up the process that will renew us, change us for the better. It is always possible to look for positive environmental features and seek them out. It is always possible to look for the sacred in all things, to consciously invite truth, beauty, and goodness into our lives. No matter how negatively conditioned your subconscious mind, the moment of decision always awaits you (here and now) and there is no determining how far you can go once you have begun. If you can think ennobling thoughts—or, better yet, accurate thoughts-- and acquire the self-discipline of meditation, there is no limit.

Because people don't always value thought, thinking as they ought, meditation can seem a chore or even punishing. But this is only because of a prior de-evaluation of the importance of the concern. That is, we attach little significance to mindfulness, and this has long been the case. If we believed as we ought, that human freedom and dignity depend very directly upon the state of our minds, we would attend to thought more, acquire more discipline in how we attend to it. Attention to conscious thought widens the "space" of consciousness. We become less and less automata, creatures of habit and the subconscious. If we exercise freedom, it isn't as bodily beings. It is as thinking, mindful beings. And without freedom, without choice, life would be a sad piece of business indeed.

At first, you will find meditation in all likelihood unpleasant. However, over time it will be a rich source of enjoyment and satisfaction. I prefer not to do what I am told with respect to meditation. I believe it is possible to be very attentive, very aware of our own minds no matter what we are doing. I don't assume any particular posture or chant. Instead, I learn to focus, to turn thought on and off (like a camera), to gain a deeper appropriation of thought and more control over it. I learn to identify the kinds of thoughts that serve me well as against those that don't. Everyone believes in technology. But the fact is that technology has left us as mindless as human beings have ever been. The key to personal and professional success is mindfulness, and this is more the case today than ever. We need clarity and the ability to think for ourselves. We need to be able to do this while median incomes are sinking (as they have been in the US over the last 30 years), while standards of living decline in the West and rise elsewhere. If we can truly think for ourselves, we will not be destined to share in this common fate. We will be able to identify opportunities of which we were previously unaware and chose differently.

I hope you see that I have wasted no time. After all, I have drawn you into the thick of an ancient debate, a debate so well-conceived millennia ago that it rages on (e.g. in the writings of Richard Dawkins as well as the post-Heideggerians). And what, you might be asking, does this have to do with love and money? Let's pause here a moment to consider.

If you are asking this question, a couple of things are already possible. It could be that you have not sufficiently established trust in me, and such reluctance is not so hard to understand. However, I doubt that this is what is centrally at stake. You purchased this book, surrendered some (albeit relatively small) portion of your hard-earned money, with no more reason to trust me than you now have. This was your decision, and if there is anything I have thus far said that has deprived you of this initial faith, to whatever degree it existed in making you part with the purchase price, it can only be that what I have said thus far does not correspond with what you hoped or expected to find, and that you see this as something of a misfortune.

You, above all, the disappointed one, I encourage to persevere and resist premature closure. Your assumptions are quite active, as they are in us all, but what I am proposing here is univocal: The unexamined assumption is both a positive hindrance and the surest sign of freedom circumscribed, of options that have gone overlooked, of possibility lost, of an unenlightened subconscious. Consider the possibility that if you are raising the "What's the point?" question now, it could be because you are unwilling to challenge your old habits of living. Old habits, once challenged, do have a way of fighting back, of attempting to regain dominance. Subconsciously we want things as they were. We want repetition. But if the societies in which we reside are characterized by unprecedented rates of change, will we not be drawn into conflict? We want the familiar, more of the same, repetition—and we can't have it. Does it not seem quite possible that this dynamic would be a most potent and widespread source of discomfort, unhappiness, even mental illness?

Another reason that you might be raising this question (What does all of this have to do with love and money?) is that I seem to be taking a detour through thought, perhaps quite speculative, and, as Emerson feared, who has time for that? "I don't want to ponder imponderables," you might be thinking: "I want to act, maybe in a very big way."

Allow me to remind you of the performative dimension of this book. Whether or not you see the relevance of what has been said thus far, my promise remains that you will. I ask that for a moment you suspend your assumptions, bracket your expectations, leave the ponderable and the value of pondering to me, and simply attend to what is being said. The great psychotherapist Milton

Erickson once made a similar request of his patients. He asked them to attend and "Let my voice go with you." To let a voice go with you is to be open to guidance, to be educable. It is more: It is to store up treasures in the head. It is to be a light unto oneself, one's own best guide. To decide *in advance* that time is being wasted is evidence of the opposite, an uneducable mind. Those who guide themselves best are always gathering information, accepting counsel.

The first habit of mind that is worth deliberate cultivation is the ability to linger, to turn oneself over to something for its own sake, the ability to put aside strict considerations of time (even if for only a moment). This is a requisite step toward order, stability, a more disciplined mind. As F. Scott Peck observed, what we call *love* is actually *discipline*-- a word that sounds decidedly discordant in a 21st-century context. There is no lasting love without order, self-harmony, delight in doing nothing (though not doing nothing always), sound judgment, the right habits of thought and the choices that arise upon the securest possible foundation. Love is not passion, for that comes and goes and permits no distinction between love and lust, love and selfishness, love and hate. The love that matters is that which endures, that which depends upon commitment, upon principle, upon the stability of choice given the sound judgment of a disciplined mind. And no discipline of any kind can be achieved in the absence of the ability *to linger*. To linger lovingly is to maintain a love—a capacity for enjoyment and satisfaction—that goes with you always, that is inseparable from who you are. To linger is to reside within a characteristic mood and to resist nothing.

Imagine the couple who exchange wedding vows out of a commitment to maintain henceforth the emotionally heightened state generally spoken of as love. What are the odds they will succeed? Would they make it a year without an argument and the thought "I don't love you"? This raises the question that if love is not the boom and bust of passion, what in human nature provides lastingness in this regard? The answer is principle. And I don't mean principles embraced because they have been recommended to us by friends or do-gooders or whomever. I mean principles that have been thought through and tested in your own experience, principles with the power to elevate and ennoble.

The great philosopher Nietzsche proposed what he thought the ultimate test. He even thought that it would sort the higher human being from the lower. The logic involved seems to be bunk, and it is not entirely clear that Nietzsche himself bought the argument. The reasoning goes like this: If the universe is bounded and therefore finite (as it seems it must be or it could not have begun anywhere—i.e., the big bang—and it could not end anywhere—e.g., at the furthermost expansion of the "stuff" of the big bang), given an infinite expanse of time (i.e., it seemed to Nietzsche, and many others before and since, impossible to imagine a time when time *was not* or a time when it *will be not*), all finite possibilities must exhaust themselves in the infinite, and therefore there must be eternal repetition (with countless variations). In other words and by analogy, the sides of dice are finite and, as such, there simply must be a repetition of the exact same sequences given enough throws. The same logic would apply to the whole universe, giving rise to what scientists (cosmologists) have denominated the multiverse.

Nietzsche's point? Whether you accept the logic of his argument or not—and it really makes no difference whatever—you are confronted with a question that interrogates you to the core: Would you live your life over in every detail exactly as you have lived it an infinite number of times already going forward? You must spend some time in reflection for the true depths of Nietzsche's test to break over you. If you had everything you have ever been, done, said, avoided doing, every last jot and tittle of your life not behind you but wholly before you—indeed, over and over again—could you affirm this life, embrace it forever?

If your answer is that you could not, how would you characterize those events that you would not want over again? What do they share in common that makes them unpleasant? Were they events that occurred while you were powerless, events due to thoughtlessness, recklessness, ignorance, blind obedience to the passions and desires? If any of these characterizations rings true, to what extent have these unhappy moments served as object lessons? After all, the past is not a series of stubborn facts strung on a timeline. The past is always in advance interpreted. It is a story told from a certain angle of vision, and it is as subject to revision as any other text. Were the events of our lives lived through properly the first time? Did we value them as we ought to have? How do we live our lives as if we were dying—that is, truthfully? The great thinker Heidegger spoke of being-unto-death as the source of authenticity. However, we are always in the state of being-unto-death. This is always already contained in the moment of decision. How could we decide so poorly? Nietzsche's principal interest was in ethics—or, as he put it, the values that serve life—and it will be necessary at this point to say something on the subject.

An ethical question, when it is the right one, is an opportunity to regain our freedom and, with that, our dignity. A question, even if for a moment only, holds open a "space" for honesty to happen. All manner of influences have been at work upon us since birth (this is what socialization is all about), we have had teachers and mentors, but the questions we will raise here will provide you the opportunity to think for yourself, to break free of groupthink, from what everyone simply assumes to be true. The question is the space of this freedom, for if we think as all these others do, as "everyone" does, we can never act for ourselves, achieve adult independence, be truly free.

Ethics--the study of good and evil, of right and wrong--is not a grab bag of moral claims ("Thou Shalt Not Gloat!") without rhyme or reason. It also is not ultimately an eye-of-the-beholder goose chase. In fact, the assertion that there is no objective moral truth or that ethics is in the eye of the beholder is a claim asserting a universal ethical truth. That is, it is self-contradictory.

Ethics is a rational reflection upon good and evil (without weighing in on the question of heaven or hell, angels and demons). The good, it must be made clear from the outset, is not relative or illusory or anything of the sort. It is inescapable. Whenever a choice arises, virtually every moment of our waking lives, there is *the good*, and absolutely nothing can change this stubborn fact. If I choose X over Y, I have identified X as yielding the greater good. Without this weighing of the good in all of its degrees of better and worse, no choice could be made, and human freedom would vanish like a mirage.

The word *ethics* refers to our identification of the "good" in any given situation as well as the rationale for the identification. Consider an example.

A friend has come to your door seeking a place to hide. He says that he is being pursued by a maniac and that his life is in danger. The good, in this context, might be identified as friendship or as loyalty. If so, it is likely you will take the desperate man into your home. Let's say that this is what you do.

Sure enough, Crazy Eddie (the maniac) appears at your door. He demands that you produce your friend so that he can shoot him. As you can see, everything depends at this moment on what gets identified as the good. We know what *the good* is for the friend (staying alive and unharmed) and for Crazy Eddie (shooting your friend). But what will it be for you? Let's say that you call to mind the old adage that honesty is always the best policy, and you accordingly confess that the friend is hiding in a closet just down the hallway. Because you don't see any advantage in physically grappling with Crazy Eddie, the maniac pushes right past you and shoots and kills your friend.

At every step there has been a reflection, however brief, upon the good, the desired outcome. But it is not at all clear that the rationale at each point, the justification for choosing one good over another, was sensible. Ethics engages each of us at the level of the thought, the reasoning process, that goes into every decision we make, whether for our own happiness or that of others.

Ethical choices are not simply "in the eye of the beholder," and "how well you sleep at night" is not a consideration of ethical significance. If such commonplace beliefs were even remotely accurate, there would be so little basis for law and social order that it would all seem transparently arbitrary and pointless. But it doesn't. Individuals and corporations face indictments, lawsuits, fines, and jail sentences every day, and we distinguish between Enron and Costco, Bernard Maddox and Albert Schweitzer. We do not think the difference merely imaginary.

Since Sarbanes-Oxley (2002) and the bundled-mortgage catastrophe of 2008, momentum has been building in the general public for a higher standard of ethics in the business community. At the time of writing this book, JP Morgan faces fines in the billions of dollars, and inside traders have received significant prison sentences. From the garment industry, with its disastrous outsourcing to Bangladesh, to the great banks that fixed Libor rates, every sector of the economy has reason to be more ethically introspective than ever before. And this will not be easy. We are learning to look at things differently, and most people don't even know where to begin. We are looking for a figure in the carpet, and the figure by which your personal and professional lives will become one life again, infinitely rich, stands forth before the perception informed by the new thoughts that I would now have you think, the thoughts that will lead us to rigorously question our assumptions about what constitutes thought as such.

But perhaps I have now gone too far too fast. After all, many people won't even follow me through the supporting example of Emerson presented above. How many will endure—

continue to abide, linger with--my invocation of thought directed to thought? It is easy to forget all that I have said about freedom, choice, and opportunity. And if you have in fact forgotten, if you weren't really attending and thus missed the point, ask yourself what it was that made your interest wander. Was it that something ridiculous or superfluous was mentioned and you quite rightly tuned it out? But how could you know? I have no doubt that what I am saying here is counterintuitive, but what is the alternative? Would you like me to say that, after a long career, I have learned nothing and that I have no more refined beliefs today than when I was a boy or a young man, that there is no reason to revise what you are convinced of now? But if there is no need for revision, why am I appealing to you at all? What would be the difference between what one knows at the end of a long career as against at the start? If what I say now only lifts you from your seats to clap, to laud me and my wisdom, won't it all have been a travesty? You have only identified what in some recess of the mind you already recognize and at some level know. If the thoughtful foundation for the exercise of freedom, judgment and choice is a matter of indifference, we are no more responsible for our actions than the psychotic. The mindless, like children and idiots, can never really be held accountable. We have no more control over our own destiny than over the winds. We will think just as everyone else does, swim the common cultural pool, and never once exercise autonomy. Again, if at some level you already know what I know after a long career, so much so that you can applaud it as true, I have contributed nothing, only confirmed you in your *modus operandi*. And just such affirmation is what people want. The subconscious wants it. It wants to hear our own beliefs repeated.

People in the West, and much of Asia too, have come to click along at a rapid pace. I only ask that you slow yourself down for a moment. My McDonald's CEO friend, Raymond Ku, argued on one of my recent radio shows that China is not being Westernized, and yet in the same show he spoke of the constraints that have come to affect his writings. (Raymond is a well-published author of fiction and non-fiction.) He told me on the air that the Chinese no longer have the patience or time to read a full-length novel. As such, he has had to adapt. He writes short stories that are published in Chinese newspapers. Only this will the bulk of the Chinese audience take the time to read—something that is read because time permits.

Is this not American time? And if the Chinese are on American time, will they be *themselves* still, on this radically different schedule? If the pace of life changes in China due to modernization, does this not represent a cultural change of the profoundest kind? Are the Chinese people not changed by Watt and the steam engine, by the industrial revolution that first swept England and then the whole of the West?

I understand that China yet in many ways sees itself as the Middle Kingdom, and I think Mr. Ku was entirely forthright. Culture matters in China, so much so that even when it has been lost, the loss itself is unthinkable. For all I know, something very like this might be at the root of uprisings in the Islamic world, a resistance to the modernization that puts us all on the same schedule, the same life rhythm, that puts us on clock time rather than nature time, mathematical time rather than actual time, sterile time that is countable rather than seasonal time (full of shadows and landscapes, summer days and bleak mid-winter). This is part of the exchange I had with Raymond on the radio.

McCarty: My guest today is Raymond Ku, the former CEO of McDonald's in Taiwan. He is a writer. He has just had a short story published in China. He is a poet. He has translated children's stories in English. He is a well-known painter. In fact, he is something of a Renaissance man. When Raymond and I first met, the subject of East and West came up. We talked about the difficulties of translating American English into Chinese and vice versa. Now, you oversaw the spread of McDonald's in Taiwan, and I would think that required the most extraordinary act of translation in the broadest sense. You had to translate American eat-and-run food into a Chinese idiom. Or perhaps not. Maybe China has become as ADHD as the United States. But historically the Middle Kingdom has been the land of patience.

Raymond Ku: McDonald's is an international phenomenon, an icon. In Paris, near the Sorbonne, people attended the McDonald's dressed up. The same thing happened in Taiwan. I think the appeal is simple—the American, modern mentality with no bullshit. This value has become more widespread, all across the world. We don't have time to devote to any one thing. We want to be able to do a lot of stuff. Other people in the world want to say, "We can be as speedy, as multi-channeled, as Americans."

McCarty: The founding brothers of McDonald's in California wanted to standardize the production of food, create something like the assembly line.

Ku: Yes. And they also saw the trend, how young people wanted to live their lives. Young people could take the food and go.

McCarty: Now the McLean burger was a failure. It was generally consider quite dry. Was that before your time with the company?

Ku: Yes. They wanted to make a burger with less fat. So they produced a 90% lean burger with 10% seaweed. The seaweed was to bind the water. The burger was too dry. It didn't taste like a juicy hamburger. McDonald's tried a few products that failed. One was pizza. They spent ten years researching pizza. They tried square pizzas, circular ones, all kinds. In blind tests, they always came out number one, on top. But somehow, when people saw it was McDonald's, they thought, "They can't be making pizza." Brand association runs very deep in people's heads.

McCarty: I wonder if China is becoming Americanized. I don't want to see the Americanization or Westernization of the globe. I think you essentially were saying that we don't eat food so much as ideas. I don't know what Coca-Cola tastes like. It has been invested with so much meaning, I guess it tastes like America. I think it was Chairman Mao who was given a Pepsi and said that it tasted like cough syrup. When I heard this, I thought, "I'll be damned. It does."

Ku: They are eating ideas, yes. The rest of the world, they all want to wear blue jeans, drink Coca-Cola, watch American movies. They want the conveniences and symbols of the US. But they are not adopting the idea, the value that is American. They are different in what drives them. We both wear blue jeans, but we may think about things quite differently in terms of priorities. To catch up with America, they do not have to go through the same growth process. They can pick the best features and directly pursue them. And they can feel materially, economically, symbolically that they are with America now. But meanwhile they have their own agenda. The next century or more will not feature one dominant power. It will be like the Internet. The Chinese or the Indian influence will be everywhere. The goods in our stores are made in China. If America wanted to attack China, they would be attacking their own lifestyle.

McCarty: You aren't worried about homogenization. I remember the first time I approached the Acropolis in Athens. It was after sundown and, as I neared it, there were the golden arches obstructing my view. But you see at work a menu. China doesn't become American. It just makes choices from the menu.

Ku: Yes. The American way, the last 200 years, learning from American successes—these factors of dominance were products of war (the world wars, the Civil War). A number of things made America very efficient, gave it an organized way of dealing with the world. This made America very successful, put a man on the Moon. It is a scientific way of dealing with reality, conquering nature. Americans became very organized, methodical, very scientific, very logical. Things are different in the East. Hong Kong University did a study about thinking. The West tends to be orderly, sequential, A, B, C, D. You understand

A and then you go to B and so on. Eastern thinking is more visual. Western languages are alphabetic. In the Orient, a linguistic character is an idea, a picture. Water looks like water, the character for mountain like a mountain. When Eastern and Western people meet to discuss business within McDonald's, they drive each other crazy. The Western people want to say, "Hey, this doesn't make sense. A plus B, etc." The Eastern people tend to say, "What about K? What happened to the K?" Because K is the only thing that matters to them. The American says, "Wait a minute. I was talking about A and B and C. How can I talk about K?" The oriental is saying, "I am at U. In my head, I have a picture. I already see A and B and C. I am at U. I see A to Z. I want to focus on F." It is visual thinking versus auditory thinking. You find things are logically quite different. In America, if you receive a gift, you are supposed to open it up and let everyone watch. In the Orient, you hide it. The attitude is, "I don't need your stuff." Social behavior is almost the exact opposite from East and West because of different value assumptions. Another example comes from when I worked in Taiwan, on major festival days. We, individually, want to give our boss presents. Because I work for him, I want to be in his good graces. In the West, the boss will make damn sure he gets a bottle of wine, something, for each employee. In China, it is the opposite.

McCarty: In China you have capitalism with a very large state component, and there has been corruption. For some time now, there has been an effort at reform. Is there a connection, culturally speaking, between this giving of gifts to the boss and the abuse of positions of power?

Ku: When we talk about rampant corruption, one must look to Chinese history. There is actually no religion in China. For generations there has been no belief system to make you think there is a heaven. There was nothing higher than the king or queen. As such, if you have any governmental position, you are to be feared and respected—because with power everything will come to you. The West has long believed in a higher power, something spiritual. But in China today, even if you are relatively low-level, you get extremely rich. Bribery, the payoff system, is a matter of course. Something else: In the West, there are relationships but business is the most important object. In the US, we accumulate good faith, trust, so that once we have done business a few times, we can become good buddies. In the Orient, you need to know the individual first. That is what is more important. You build a relationship and then you do business. What counts in China is relative position in the social hierarchy. China is a place where people are so anxious to find out how much money you make. This is a shorthand way to find out one person's position relative to another's, yours to mine. So the taxi driver will ask, "Sir, how much do you make a year?" They don't know how to treat you without knowing where you stand in the social order. They want to find out who your father was, where he went to school, where you go to school—so that they can feel comfortable having properly placed themselves with respect to you. How "I" fit in is crucial for the Chinese.

McCarty: In the United States, there is an unwillingness to even recognize hierarchy. George Washington was the only president who wouldn't shake hands with citizens. Americans today wouldn't scruple to walk up to the Queen of England and start talking—and they will also talk to a cab driver. What I don't like about all of this is the absence of the sense of being embedded in anything.

Ku: Right. You can see it that way, but there is also something positive about it too. Take, for example, the American ambassador to China. He was a Chinese born in America. It was reported in the papers in China that in the United States he had stopped at a Starbucks coffee, pulled out a credit card, with a discount coupon, and paid for his purchase. In China, he lost respect. You are supposed to be an official, an ambassador, and you act like that, you act like us!

McCarty: What is the problem? Is it the coupon?

Ku: No. You are supposed to act like an ambassador, someone in an important position. You can't be acting like a civilian.

McCarty: Getting your own coffee even.

Ku: Right. That is why, after being in America for a while, I get so disgusted with the Chinese police in the street, shouting at their own people like tyrants. But if they see an American visitor, they are instantly all smiles. I cannot stand that. But the fact is that they cannot be nice to the people. If they are nice, the people won't respect them. It has to be this way.

McCarty: I used to write for the White House, and I can never forget walking in for the first time and seeing how small it is. What does someone coming from China think when they see that such a central structure is so relatively modest?

Ku: That is one thing Eastern people need to learn from the West: What is the true spirit of democracy? What has made America in only 200 years such an empire? But the White House is still a majestic building. It is revered, so their reaction wouldn't be extreme. But there would be surprise. A lot of times the Chinese think that America is bigger in words than in reality. And there is something else I want to mention. Because of the teaching tradition of the West, its moral dogma and religion, the Golden Rule, etc., its people from childhood are taught good and evil, the battle between them, and so on. In the Orient, there is rarely teaching of right and wrong per se. Children will hear anecdotes from history, strategies, tactics, how to win things, how to beat other people.

McCarty: Are you saying that there is a Machiavellian quality to oriental thinking?

Ku: Right. Because of the experience of merely surviving for thousands of years, the people are very practical. They are concerned with whatever works. It is thought that there are Buddhists and Christians, but in China the real religion is whatever works. So if I am a Christian traveling through the villages and I see a Buddhist temple, I will go in there and burn some incense, just so I don't irritate some other god. What other country in the world could say, "We are Communists and also capitalist dogs!"? They are the most practical people in the world.

McCarty: I wonder if China is slowly changing. There are bloggers going to jail for human rights, political reform. There seem to be more of them and it seems they are more aggressive than ever before.

Ku: Yes. That is accurate. It is the force of people's awareness even though the government tries to block information. People travel. They get the information anyway. This cannot be stopped. This is a global trend. Even though the people are still scared shitless of the government, they get together and compare notes. The middle class is being built, however slowly and painfully. There is a drastic difference between the rich and the poor. This is still a major concern, but there is movement. Taiwan went through the same process. It became a more reasonable society, with two-party rule, democratic processes. That took about 40 or 50 years. China has to go that way, but the extreme control of the Communists slows progress down.

McCarty: China has to go that way because of the sheer number of stakeholders and the substantial stakes?

Ku: Right. A lot of the current leaders in China were educated in the West. They graduated from Harvard. They are bound to know what the society needs. The layers and layers of payoffs, the corruption is still there, but they have to do something about it.

McCarty: Right now it looks like the Chinese government is going to punish some very visible people among their own ranks so as to save the rest.

Ku: Yes.

McCarty: It's not all that unlike the US. Here all of these agencies have been set up to police companies that are "too big to fail" and some of the fines thus far sound huge, but when you consider what these same companies are making, they aren't huge at all. In fact, the companies that arguably caused the Great Recession are bigger than ever.

Ku: Yes.

McCarty: The English language is quite binary, dualistic. There is up and down, pro- and anti-, right and left. It is very black-and-white. And for a long time the world was supposedly divided up between democratic capitalists and Marxists. Today the opposition is perhaps between the forces of modernization and anti-modernization (radical Islam, for example). But how Communist was China? How real was the duality? I know that a serious effort was made under Mao to bring about true believers, but are people in China still reading Marx?

Ku: It is like Russia. There are people who miss Communist rule, especially those who feel that life today is too chaotic to manage. Maybe they are not among those who gain or profit very much. They miss the old order. The Mao revivalists will not prevail because so many more people have made economic gains, have come to control a bit more of their own fate. Hopefully, the people who miss the old order will not take over and exercise influence.

McCarty: In the West, there was this understanding of a monolithic Communist threat. Henry Kissinger spoke of linkage within an overarching policy of containment. Wherever Communism rears its head, the US is going to hold the line or, if the president is Ronald Reagan, push back, fund proxy armies, and so on. Now that was a delusion with disastrous consequences. It didn't, for instance, turn out that the Soviet Union had the kind of ties to the North Vietnamese that Kissinger thought.

Ku: Right. The Chinese people throughout the years have survived many tyrants. We still survive because the Chinese are, at bottom, very pragmatic. You can control the Chinese, kill them for twenty or fifty years, but they will still survive.

McCarty: When you are in Oakbrook, Illinois, at McDonald's corporate headquarters.

Ku: I started in Oakbrook. I worked in Oakbrook for ten years and then was sent to Taiwan to take over there.

McCarty: For a time there was a war raging between McDonald's and Burger King. I remember going into a Burger King that actually had Ronald McDonald in a casket with a gigantic ketchup-covered French fry through his heart. What did McDonald's do right that Burger King did wrong?

Ku: Consistency. Quality consistency. McDonald's invested in their people, in much longer cycles. Their employees were much more disciplined and serious. So food quality, people quality, organizational tenacity.

McCarty: If you stick it out at McDonald's and do a good job, you can go places. There are rich managers of McDonald's franchises, right?

Ku: Yes, of course.

McCarty: I have to say something about the Beijing Olympics. I have never seen synchronization, group discipline, taken that far. The May Day parade in the Soviet Union was always the display of missiles and the US got the message. Was China with the Olympics sending the American audience a message? And if so, what was the message?

Ku: Not only America, the world. China has learned in recent years about theater, packaging and drama. The whole country was behind the Olympics. Enormous amounts of money were spent on two shows. The selection process went on for four or five years. The people performing Kung Fu were from the military academy—all guys, 2000 of them, all exactly 5' 7". It is national pride, but China wants to show the world their force. It isn't the John Wayne or the Rambo approach, big guns and muscles. The Chinese want to show you the power in the masses.

McCarty: I can only imagine what the Chinese made of a swaggering character like George Bush.

Ku: Yes. But they had seen enough Western movies to know what to make of him. There is this American mentality, one man killing great numbers. If you go too far with this, obviously, it becomes a joke in the eyes of the Chinese.

McCarty: Now you recently published a short story in China. It appeared in the newspapers.

Ku: Yes. In China, people will not take the time to read a novel, a whole book. They prefer something short in the newspaper.

McCarty: American newspapers 100 years ago commonly featured short stories.

Ku: In Taiwan, the young people read more, the college and high school kids. Most people in Taiwan don't read literature any more. They read practical things—about health, investments, etc. Fiction is rarely read. 90% of readers of fiction are under the age of 20. The lifestyle has become very fragmented. Everyone wants to accomplish so many different things, and the people don't have much time to read anyway. A novel is harder to sell than short stories.

****

I stand on the verge. Those of you who have grasped what I have said will already know that. I stand on the verge, asking you to consider things that might seem hard. I stand on the verge and ask you to linger, to pause, to remain awhile, to suspend the hurry, to make the choice—the thought-induced decision to make a choice and effect it—to take your foot from the pedal and slow yourself down, to shut your inner jackrabbit down, if only for the moment. If you are still with me, you have passed something of the test, and my job now is only to encourage you to listen, to persevere. Nothing said here cannot be evaluated immediately against your own experience, and we already know that clock time is wholly impersonal, that it is a "time" that leaves us out of all consideration. Despite Mr. Ku's assurances to the contrary, it seems to me that China is now on the American schedule. The Chinese are learning to think like Westerners, and everything else (values, preferences, ideals) will shift accordingly. The appeal of McDonald's around the world is far from benign. Mr. Ku mentioned it all: chronic hurry, multitasking, consumerism, the rat race, chaos, social upheaval, the coarsening of literary tastes.

Do we really want to see the four corners of the globe alight with the fires of the industrial revolution? Do we really believe in the desirability—or even the physical possibility—of endless economic growth? Has our scientific-technological mindset really proved so successful—not in lengthening life but deepening its significance? Do we really want to be so goddamn practical, so multitasked, so constantly distracted, so busy? Do we want to see the endless expansion of technological might, even if it means the end of all life on Earth? Do we want to be dragged helplessly wherever technology blindly takes us or come to know more pervasively human decision making, the exercise of judgment, a bit more control of our own destiny? How far do we want to take standardization? To appreciate this, think about it in just one of its aspects, clock time. Think about the emptying predominance of the quantitative over the qualitative.

Perhaps the greatest force for homogenization by way of globalization is clock time. In other words, the forces driving globalization extend back centuries and elude any simple point or moment of origination. Indeed, the attempt to impose order onto time is doubtless coincident with the emergence of life itself. With the recognition of regularities in the Sun and stars, and especially the phases of the Moon (c. 30,000 BC), human beings have endeavored to represent the movement of time or change, and from this effort it was a relatively short step to representation as measurement. However, the globalization so characteristic of Western history since the Renaissance has achieved a homogenizing acceleration that in itself poses grave dangers. We are witnessing changes of a kind that the Chinese will not outwait and triumph over, their cultural identity intact.

While it must always remain somewhat notional, a regulative ideal, "natural" time is steadily eclipsed by clock time, by the time that uproots one (and all) from "earth" in the ascension toward the fullest possible evacuation of time, the demarcation of time that is also its purest nullification. The distinction between "natural" or "earth" time as against clock time must be understood concretely. So, for instance, regularities do not in and of themselves imply quantification. Seasonal rains, the flooding of rivers, all manner of recurring phenomena have long been attributed to the activity of the gods, whose good will was sought in ceremonies of propitiation. That is, the gods were the upholders or disruptors of the regularities upon which life itself depended, and belief in the god served as a conceptual brake. It isn't possible to dwell upon the gods of nature in any devout way, to maintain piety, while seeking out an impersonal causal mechanism subject to mathematical formulation. And the word *formulation* is itself a milestone in the transition from the worship of time (and more widely than merely in the figure of Chronos and so on) to its measurement.

Formulation derives from the Latin stem *formula*, meaning "form, draft, contract, regulation; rule, method." In other words, it had yet to take on the connotation of precise, exact or economical expression. This latter usage seems to date from the late 18th century. However, in this same respect, Thomas Carlyle's definition ought to be borne in mind, "the rule slavishly followed without understanding." What is at stake here is much more than "mere semantics." Globalization transpires against a horizon that contains its own intelligibility, but to understand it the intelligibility that makes it possible must be laid bare. When Raymond Ku spoke of the Western mind as methodical, scientific, logical, as seeking to master nature, he doubtless was correct. But it is this same way of thinking that poses the single greatest danger, to us as societies and individuals.

The gap that yet exists between the Latin formula and the Carlylean is the advent of the promise for the mathematization of all phenomena, and the exemplary figure in this regard is Descartes. It was Descartes who concluded beyond all doubt, or so he had it, that external reality consisted of nothing but extension, a circumstance that made it the perfect candidate for mathematical expression, pure translation into numbers, without loss or remainder. So it is Descartes who formulates the theological dream of Galileo and then Newton, the decoding of the mind of God and His creation as math, and introduces it into natural philosophy or science. It is at this point, given the Cartesian coordinates that can place a cannonball right on the desired spot, that clock time shows itself most dramatically, for the quantification of space turns out as well to be that of time. Objects in the extension that is space move, and this movement is what Galileo expressed as 32 feet per second squared and Newton as the universal law of gravitation. Time, it was thought, could be represented as an infinitely divisible line. Time and space were mathematic-geometric phenomena.

The decisive intellectual movement occurs within representation, as a shift in habits of representation. The nature god foreclosed the possibility for either hermetically sealing the divine and the earthly against each other, for rendering them mutually exclusive in terms of temporality, and for thinking of regularity as numerical purity or emptiness. The movement that occurs is an emptying, a rarefaction. As time becomes unit, each self-identical and identical to every other, all distinguishing content falls away. When time is not that of the famine or the feast or the hunt or the harvest, clock time obtains as the purity of a translation that is perfect, without excess or loss, because nothing is translated, because time itself, as it were, falls outside the translation entirely. We, and with us the rest of the globe, come to occupy this null "space," a barren emptiness that is even visible in our aesthetic (e.g. our preference for the straight lines and semi-transparency of the skyscraper, the architecture of seeing in and through all things, of complexity reduced to constitutive atoms or to numbers). Our aesthetic is as spare and minimal as our belief that nothing will remain hidden in the natural world is an absolute article of faith. Science will disclose all, and in art we anticipate the visibility of all things.

With the mathematical representation of time, the technology of measuring time became synonymous with time itself. We came to speak of devices that "keep time." The Church conceived of a calendar that would keep time in the form of the massive volume of math called *On the Revolutions of the Celestial Spheres* by a Polish priest, Copernicus. So as our technologically enhanced powers of keeping time grew, the certainty of time as clock time deepened. We even envisioned launching clocks at different speeds and calculating the velocity-induced curvature of time. And it is this mastery of time via a mathematical imposition that lies at the absolute foundation of globalization and promises a homogenization of an apocalyptic sort. Clock time has no bearing whatever on the manner in which we exist, the "pacing" we share with the natural world and that we ought to share with each other. Clock time uproots each and every one of us, and it makes the attainment of purpose more difficult than ever. It offers us life without the rhythm of a pulse.

In a moment, I am going to address the subject of *your* purpose. You are free to recoil—in fact, free to do as you like— but if you turn away now, just now, I do wonder. I can to some degree understand why you might not take my counsel on faith, why you might not care to be led through Emerson and Nietzsche, why you might see this as a circuitous path and maybe a waste of time. I have some sympathy for that sort of reaction. But if this kind of reaction remains, and only you can know, when I address the subject of purpose, my brow furrows and I am genuinely concerned, alarmed even. What does math have to do with purpose? What does nature and how we understand it have to do with purpose? Everything, I say. Purpose is only sustained in terms of the object of its intentions, and how objects in general (nature, the world, space and time) are understood percolates up into every consideration. Nothing is more fundamental.

I am engaging you—here and now—on this page. I approach you more closely than I could in any PowerPoint presentation. And whatever your reaction, whatever the assumptions (of truth) that enter into your reaction, it remains within your power to affirm this reaction, for which you have yet little warrant, but then you must put this book aside and put the test I have so painstaking designed for you aside as well. I speak of purpose, and I do not pretend that this is a neutral subject, so close by its very nature to indifference that one can respond or not, ostensibly without making a difference. We are so used to disappointments, to promises deferred and ultimately unfulfilled. Don't you remember that "You may already have won a million dollars"? This Publisher's Clearing House pitch line was only the most obscene enunciation of an absolute staple of American life, the empty promise.

What if purpose is not the pith and marrow of our existence? The problem is not having a purpose. It is losing it. Purpose can get wrung out of us. A famous study was once conducted of children aged seven and eleven. The seven-year-olds, when asked to produce a rendering of their world, used a wide range of colors, producing green grass and silvery moons. The eleven-year-olds were five times as likely to employ only black and white. One can only hope that more cannot be read into this study than at first appears, that eleven-year-olds do not in fact experience their environments in this deeply impoverished fashion. But I suspect the process that results in this impoverishment is well under way. More than that, I suspect it has been underway for a very long time. I do know that walking the dog under the blue vault of a June morning was an adventure at six. At thirty-six, no adventure. I want the dog to shit so I can return home and read the paper. Indeed, this sensible decay is almost universal. But has nothing been lost, and why does this decay occur? Charles Dickens attributed his imaginative genius to never having forgotten what it was like to be a child. Maybe the ideas that get into our heads while we are "socialized" get in the way, perhaps because they are bad ideas joined to bad ways of thinking and bad habits of thought. Perhaps even our misunderstanding of thought itself is a genuine part of the problem. Perhaps our subconscious has been hijacked by the crowd, by "everyone." Perhaps the world goes monochromatic because we think from the common pool, something into which everyone—from the sickest to the most saintly—makes a contribution.

I suppose I could sit down and break up with my girlfriend in a long and regretful (or at least considerate) 19th-century sort of letter. Or, rather than evade the full import of my actions, I could do it as it has been done time out of mind, face to face. Today I can zip off a succinct text message or two and officiate over a rather complete de-actualization of what I am in fact doing, with respect to myself and the other person. We grow up differently now. We reach puberty at an earlier age (whether due to hormone-injected cows or not, I leave for others). But we come of age spiritually later than ever before, and most of us not at all. There is no natural mechanism by which growing older translates into advanced wisdom. Growing older, as we have grounds to know, is in fact, for the vast majority of us, a deadening, a coarsening; it is a "space" for losing ourselves in a limitless labyrinth of rituals and routines, for self-sacrifice of the most agonizing and bootless kind.

This last point cannot be overstated, for it is exactly what we then do to our children.

It is as if with growing up most of us in the contemporary world enter into a radically different relationship to purpose. We once knew what we were about so well that when it came to entertaining ourselves we made up all the rules. You be the dragon. I'll be the knight. The tree will be the castle, and we shall see who takes it. In fact, children's games are typically more elaborate, much more. But what happens at 25 or 30? Why does the question "What will we do tonight?" rain down anxiety upon all involved? We could rent a movie, go bowling, hit a restaurant. We do the things everyone does, and have we anything like the number of options or the same freedom of choice we once knew? If not, does it come as any great surprise that purpose turns its Bartleby head to the wall and dies?

The great thinker Heidegger described the danger in terms of what he called "idle talk" (what gets said by just "everyone," what "everyone" knows) and the "one" (the crowd). "It is idle talk…that facilitates the intractable domination of the 'one.' 'One' inherently implies 'nobody.' Talk of this kind is distinguished by the lack of any original appropriation of what it is 'about,' and through so-called verbal thinking [mindlessly following the words, the binary oppositions, the old logic embedded in the language], which has surrendered to the power of certain verbal phrases, it may also pervade and govern the treatment of problems within scientific disciplines. In chugging along in language, uprooted *Dasein* [the human being] secures a reputation and legitimacy [both false] for itself through the public realm of the 'one'." Math is a language, and it is one we treat unlike the others (the truth of French versus, say, the truth of German or English), as if it weren't simply another semiotic invention with its own peculiar history but rather as if it came to us in a ball of fire. Math is the language that so neatly fits its referent—the things out there in the world—it requires no translation, which of course is nonsense.

Allow me to make a confession. When I was 16, I went away from home to college. This was not because I was an excellent student. I was expelled from a private Catholic high school. As such, there was no choice but to attend the public school for senior year. However, my girlfriend was graduating in December, and there was no way she was going to go to college without me. (We were in love. It was the real thing, as eternal as the stars, or so we thought. There is one thing a 16-year-old almost never knows: his or her own perspective, his or her peculiar take on things as merely one among many possible. Meta-consciousness is rare at any age, among teens almost nonexistent.) So with the unalloyed audacity of youth, I approached Mr. Harris, the longsuffering academic counselor at our high school, and told him that I simply must be graduated by Christmas. I don't know whether an aura of trouble hung about my ears and that this lent him motivation, but he actually granted my request. I have never since inquired into the legality or formal appropriateness of his decision. Naturally, I was delighted.

My girlfriend and I went off to college, took all the same classes, sat next to each other in every one, and broke up at the end of the term. But something had been inaugurated in me that would not flare up only to burn out like puppy love. I had a purpose. Whether the deep motive was to exact personal vengeance upon what I doubtless considered an obnoxious institution or a declaration that turn and turnabout are alike fair play, I have never discovered, but I was determined to become a teacher. My deep motivation didn't matter. The prospect of becoming a teacher filled my life with excitement.

I don't believe I will ever forget the feeling. It has always convinced me that it is possible to identify the purpose that will sustain one. One, of course, can never count on forever. I did in fact become a teacher and remained one for 25 years, and then lost interest and decided to do something else. I had no regrets whatever. If we change while clinging rigidly to an obsolete purpose, we ourselves become obsolete, bored, zestless and Starbucks-guzzling. If we think only as language permits, carried along by it, we lose ourselves in the empty "one." I want to get out of bed in the morning like a missile, not like the condemned. I prefer energy internally generated over the perpetual, addictive hunt for stimulants (music, TV, caffeine, shopping). It comes as no surprise to me that people are guzzling Starbucks coffee as if their lives depended upon it, that Starbucks is one of the most successful companies in the world. Perhaps in some small way coffee comes to stand in for actual purpose.

But let's linger here for a moment. Allow me to pose a question to which you most certainly have the answer: Do you get up in the morning like a missile? If not, you have lost your way and you are no longer your own master. Something other than a purpose peculiar to you is the driving force. But this word, this "something," is no comfort. One wants to know how to get back on track, and to know that one must have some idea of how one gets off track. The latter is not a detour or scenic route to the former.

Some people suffer clinical depression. They go to a psychotherapist or a psychiatrist for help. However, I believe in a low-grade depression that never shows up in clinical form. It is often the product of having made all kinds of compromises with life, of acting on the belief that it is easier (and hence better) to stay just as I am than to embrace something new, to make different kinds of choices. I believe it is built into our cultural experience together, one I would describe as being alone together. We have erased all power and majesty and beauty and depth from the Earth and sky and have replaced it with the highly dubious conviction that all is being revealed to us thanks to science and technology. The curtain falls from all things and everything isn't merely naked, even the nakedness is naked—like bodies without skin.

If you have ever had a brush with death, you might be able to relate. When the reality of death dawns, as it has on me more than once, I don't hope for more life, for on and on. I would prefer to die right, following my own enthusiasm, my own agenda. I have come to believe the cliché that it isn't the length of a life that counts, but the quality. Show me one late afternoon, on an autumn day perhaps, when the distant whistle of a train makes me aware of being alone in a terrific space, a person all here and now, with this moment spread out before me with its *more*—its more depth, more beauty, more truth than anyone could ever express—beneath an infinite expanse of sky; show me this, all in a flash, and I will lay down and die. TV commentators and actuaries operate on the assumption so widely shared that "progress" is all about health and length of life. Entertainment moguls tell me that it is all about youth and coolness and intense pleasures. The prophets of scientific salvation tell me that this is a new and better age because we somehow know better, can make better things, and perhaps one day will reproduce consciousness on a hard drive, become gods unto ourselves, self-givers of immortality. But I don't believe in god or immortality, and I wouldn't want them regardless. I do, however, believe in the highest value, the sacred. I believe in it not because it makes me feel good, though it does, but because I have experienced it for a lifetime, like the nose on one's face. It is that which goes overlooked just before all the colors fade.

What happens if one believes in none of my claims? Or, what happens if one does believe in many of them, but is unable to bracket dissenting beliefs for the course of this book? The seven-year-olds painting in color, the eleven-year-olds in black-and-white—what if nothing has gotten into the water, what if the difference that makes all the difference resides in what we believe and then in the ability to regain control of this? Our beliefs need not just happen to us. We can care about them so much that they become the objects of genuine interrogation. Only in this way, I would argue, do our beliefs become supple and interesting. But the content of our beliefs matters too, and we should argue—argue always, interrogate, ponder, look on.

Here is my thesis: If you have lost your purpose, no longer arise from bed like a missile, your beliefs are not what you think they are. That is, the thoughts that rationalize your going about day upon day in the same way, all without heart, are false—even to your own experience, for this experience is telling you, even if only in a low-grade way, that you have chosen a course which is not for you. Imagine something deeper than cognition, something that might be invoked here as *awareness* or attunement, nothing deficient for its being less thoroughly concept-governed. At some level you are aware that you are not an island, but that you also cannot exist as a reflex of the crowd. You have to have a degree of independence to exercise some control over your own life. Clock time plunges us all into the crowd and removes time as a dimension in which we truly find our individuality, in which the separateness of our personhood—always relative—is on its own, its proper schedule. We can't find our purpose if the time in which we would live it is not our own.

According to research, and common sense, students who know what they will do with their education after they have received their degree are much less likely to drop out of school, as much as four times less likely. The research is interesting and worth consulting, but this was something I already knew from personal experience. I have spent years of my life in graduate school. However, I cannot recall a single occasion when I was happy to be in class. I hated formal classroom instruction then and I hate it now. Given this, one might wonder how I survived graduate school at all, or why I would even have made the attempt. I was able to do it—twice, two doctoral programs—because I always knew *what I wanted when I was done*, because the outcome was in very clear focus and the steps leading from where I was at any given time to where I ultimately wanted to be were ones that inspired me with confidence—by virtue of their very visibility.

As the great thinker Alain Badiou and many others have demonstrated with exceptional rigor, things considered in isolation are always thereby fictionalized. So it would be wrong to think about purpose as if it were simply a subjective affair, a certain characteristic or human propensity. Purpose is that which is always out beyond the individual. Purpose does not belong to a person in the same way one's limbs or organs do. Purpose is not merely about "finding oneself" or working oneself up into a state of enthusiasm. Purpose always depends as an inner state on an outer state, the clarity of the object to which it is directed, and only in this way is it sustained. Purpose is not chiefly what exists at two terminal points (the human self and the object), but what emerges in *the relationship between* the two.

Purpose is always engaged, drawing one out of the tightly circumscribed fictive self. Purpose is always directed to an end that is not it, but inseparable from it. It is always a purpose toward…genuine love, material well-being, the acquisition of manners by one's children and so on. Purpose is always multiple. It is inclined toward an end or goal that it itself is not but without which it couldn't be. It is maintained in the context of what is actual, of what goes forward in the world we know, or it is self-defeating, chimerical, delusional—something that cannot be maintained given an adequate sense of reality. And, it needn't be said, purposes devoid of precisely this context are mad (though even mad purposes have ends and fantastic contexts).

Purpose is best thought of not as an entity or an emotional state but as a kind of instantaneous movement through the world, our surroundings taken in total, and defined with respect to an end or goal. Purpose is a way of being attuned to our environment in such a manner that we know how to move through it so that the movement through it takes on added satisfaction. I say that it is an instantaneous movement because it contains an element of spontaneity, and it simply is not possible to make an appointment with spontaneity. I say it is instantaneous because it arises out of the total context (the opportunities and obstacles the world presents) and not some isolated thing or another. Purpose is not purpose except as it naturally arises. The moment it is forced, once I no longer believe in the steps that would take me to the goal, once I no longer believe that the goal can be realized, purpose vanishes—because it has never been anything separate from these other "things." Nothing like scientific causality is involved (i.e., billiard ball A strikes billiard ball B causing B to move).

Our culture and, as such, we ourselves are quite good at analytic thinking, the approach to problems and things that breaks them down, takes them apart, considers them in isolation, and then reassembles them. In fact, this is a model of thinking (transmitted from Pythagoras and Descartes to Einstein and so-called common sense) that is rapidly being adopted the world over in the concrete form of automation, modernization, globalization, and the consequences have been and promise to be nothing short of catastrophic. My claim here is not that analytic thinking is an absurdity. It is rather that analytic thinking does not suffice, that one should be practiced in another style of thinking. Only then can you, as master of two styles of thought, make a judgment, immediately experience the difference, know when one approach is preferable to the other, and how and when they ought to be combined. This difference is the one the famous thinker Georg Hegel underscored in his understanding/reason opposition. He saw the distinction as rife with world-historical importance, and he was right.

The phrase "style of thinking" may at first seem hopelessly abstract, but it is important that we flesh everything out, that we linger with these abstractions until we see how they make traction in our actual lives. The most pervasive and widely considered effective psychotherapy today is called DBT or dialectical behavioral therapy. DBT is illustrative. The emphasis is upon, among other things, styles of thought, the crucial importance of both the way we think and of what we think, the form and the content.

The word *dialectical* refers very precisely to the non-analytical mode of thinking I have just mentioned. It recognizes that there are "things" but that they are never ultimately isolated. One can try to think the singularity associated with the big bang of cosmological theory, the point so incredibly compact and dense that it exploded into the universe—matter, energy, space and time. One can try to think it, but one cannot. One cannot think the singularity that is everything and yet entirely environed by nothing. If one thinks it, one thinks it incorrectly—as already in space. But as the origin of space it cannot already be in space. It has to be "situated" wholly in the nothing, and that means that the nothing too would have to be…something.

The ability to think, to achieve clarity on how one does think, to identify a style of thought (analytic) as against another style of thought (dialectical)—these are crucial if one is to exercise choice, live deliberately, abide within a "zone" of purpose. In the case of the students I have already mentioned in terms of graduation rates, the key factors were clarity of the goal (the "for what?" of purpose) and the degree of conviction concerning the steps in achieving it (the "how?" of purpose).

One might think that arrival at this kind of clarity would be an enormous chore. It is not. It is a chore only if one does not experience its inevitability. If the account I have provided of purpose seems merely one of many possible (or entirely wrongheaded), the way to clarity will prove a horrendous struggle, one not worth undertaking. Clarity must bear its value on its forehead. Its indispensability must be so patently obvious as to put any question regarding it beyond all reasonable doubt. It is not in these circumstances a chore. It is like food or water. It is simply what one must have, and in this light the process of achieving it becomes extraordinarily interesting—ultimately, a source of genuine passion in its own right.

This is a process you can observe right now. If at this moment you really do see that there is no substitute for clarity, you will find right now that you have more of it than you had before. The mere recognition of clarity in its intrinsic value induces a degree of clarity, clarity concerning a first principle (its necessity). People fly by the seat of their pants, without warrant. No one would board a plane with such a pilot. No one would want to defend oneself in a court of law before a jury that was operating on impressions, hunches, feelings and the like. We want justice to be a matter of reason, of due consideration of the evidence (not analytically but dialectically, as it forms an integrated whole) given the ability to draw a sound inference.

So we have come to a fork in the road. Some readers will recognize the supreme importance of clarity. Others will not. In either case, a truly significant insight has been won. Those dedicated to clarity will probably read on and perhaps come to explore all of the possibilities, undreamt of, that emerge as a result. Those who don't believe in the need for clarity can stop reading here. But, whether they know it or not, they will not walk away with nothing. They will now know beyond all doubt that muddle is alright, that they prefer a style of thinking that is without rigor, that they are comfortable winging it, believing the kinds of things that just "everyone" believes, making choices that aren't well considered, living life in hopes of chance breaks and good fortune (rather than via deliberation and realistic goal setting). They will know that they have yoked their cart to Lady Luck and are in for a wild ride, and for drama freaks and chaos-mongers this is quite a lucid insight. So it is a good thing to have gained clarity about the desirability of a neglected and unfocused mind, but there is nothing more to say to one with this precise kind of clarity. It will always speak for itself.

Sustained purpose depends on clarity. The goal that only exerts power on purpose to the degree that it is defined—clear, realistic, achievable—is always available, but we are not always available to it; we are not always in tune with ourselves or our surroundings, whether because we have gone on automatic pilot, because we have opted for safety and security over richness of life and meaning, because we have enslaved ourselves to obligation, because we have worn textbook lenses for so long that we can no longer take an honest view of ourselves, because we have done the wrong thing and it is too painful to confess it to ourselves, because of an ego-driven life, because we have enslaved ourselves to the clock, and so on.

Our language and culture are dualistic. We believe in professional and personal lives and that they are somehow separate or even opposed to each other. Everyone behaves as if there is in fact this division, as if it were natural. (We warn people "Don't take your work home with you" or "Keep your personal life out of the workplace.") But it would be a mistake to assume that this duality has much basis outside our cultural assumptions. The purpose that supports us in one area of life is required in all the others as well. Our maps are always necessary, but they get in the way when we assume that they correspond to the territory in any far-reaching way.

Nonetheless, the imaginary opposition of the personal and the professional often proves decisive. We very commonly have it that our loved ones (spouses, children, friends) provide us the bedrock or foundational purpose for everything we do. Often this belief lends itself to a certain willingness in "our professional lives" to become sacrificial lambs. Our careers are compromised. They are no longer fulfilling, but the duality of personal and professional allows us, or so it is thought, to shoulder the lifeless burden of the workaday world in the name of love for family and friends. I have known people in various parts of the world who give precious little thought even to what kind of work they do. They will take any kind of job, as long as the pay is sufficient, and frequently they can persevere in this way for years in the knowledge that once the workday is over an evening in the pub awaits them. I needn't say anything about the per capita murder rate in places like Glasgow, Scotland.

Not for a moment is it my intention to oversimplify. There exist all manner of rationales for why people make the choices they make. Nonetheless, there are certain "fault lines" that we must observe, just as we must share a certain common understanding to use the same language, take note of the same norms, protocols, prohibitions. Another "fault line" that shows itself in tandem with the dubious duality of the "personal versus professional" is our widespread conception of a job as a "place" to hunker down. Jobs are scarce. Globalization means that employers depress wages as far as possible and exercise employee-directed loyalty little or not at all. One gets a job and hunkers down in it because every other kid in Asia wants the same job and landing a good one is parsed out as a feat worthy of Houdini or the Chinese syndicate. After all, read the newspapers. Read the statistics on median incomes. This is a stubborn fact of 21st-century life. Or so people think.

It would be easy to say that it is indeed, for that is what everyone is saying. But this is not something I would place in the category of "fact." I would distinguish between the map and the territory, and I would treat the "fact" of our economic situation in the relationship between the two. That is, I would think about it dialectically. Our notions of how things ought to unfold—our expectations, wants, desires, sense of normality—have already in advance entered into all of these so-called facts. There still exists the tendency to think of ourselves as employees in search of employers, as dependent upon companies to supply the jobs that we need. Yet this is the merest habit of thought, one (it is true) that is perpetuated by almost all of our institutions of education, civic life and government. One has been warned sufficiently: Do not go to college and major in art if you want later to escape poverty or live comfortably. Instead of consulting your peculiar mix of talents and interests, study software design or engineering, the hard sciences, medicine. And this advice is of course based on the dualistic assumption that if you must choose between your head and your heart, between the professional and the personal, between money and love—always choose the former. But such a logic makes no sense if the dualism invoked is imaginary. It also makes no sense if the supply of software designers expands, via more graduates or a more widely available visa, for then their wages will go down as surely as those of the auto worker at GM.

There has never been as much opportunity in human history as there is at this moment. But to navigate the territory in which such opportunity resides, we will have to put away our old maps. The terrain is relatively new—that of infinite connectivity. Artists no longer require monsters of publishing like Time Warner or Random House. Historians no longer require a life in academia. Speakers of multiple languages no longer require an embassy. We have witnessed the most massive decentralization of all time and we have already achieved a level of technological advancement that absolutely insures that decentralization will continue. The notion of companies that are "too big to fail" belongs not to the future but to the past. The high noon of capital centralization in the form massive multinational corporations is passed. The war between the titans of industry today, a war that ranges on almost every continent, is a death struggle. And the tides of history do not favor the old behemoths.

Again, the dualism of head and heart is false. One can't choose one over the other because one can't have one without the other. The undirected mind (unfocused, without purpose) is of no more use than a bad heart, than stupid obedience to appetites and inclinations. Any work that is without satisfaction for the worker incites revolt. The slave is perhaps the best illustration. The slave will work, especially if his very existence is put at risk, but he will always have an eye out for freedom. That is, he will always seek the actualization of his own purposes, this most fundamental of inclinations. The antebellum dread of Nat Turner-style slave insurrection was quite real, and would end up a major *casus belli*.

We love, work and play all out of a sense of something truly basic—care. When we care, we attend in the moment to that which is most significant. The baby, the cat or dog—these have to be attended to on their own schedules. They must eat when they are hungry. Anything else would immediately suggest an absence of care, and care requires above all else *attention*. We attend, make ourselves available, focus upon, linger with, abide by— whatever it is we care for. This is what our spouses want, our children, our pets, our friends—and they want it above all else. Somewhere in our collective past we have forgotten that the same must be the case in our work, that work must be done with care, and that there are no substitutes for it. Care in the form of attention is its own guarantee of authenticity. The time has to be taken to attend, abide, linger, to make available. And in an ADHD culture, the first casualty is care—living life at the proper speed. The pace of a culture is the single most significant feature of it, and it is for this reason that Plato spoke of taking control of a city-state by way of its music. Attention requires its own span, its own temporality. We cannot pencil in "quality time." This conception of time negates all quality.

People once lived seasonal lives. They belonged to the natural world and they didn't need to be told. But over the last few centuries (a veritable blink of the eye for *homo sapiens*), man has diverged and come to live according to clock time—the time of uniformity, of standardization, quantified time. And with this uniformity, human productivity gets measured out like cloth, as if by the yard (e.g. X units of labor at Y per hour). We set aside time for work and time for play, quality time for family and friends, burdensome time for chores and doctor appointments, time for school and for fun. But the temporal framework for all of this activity trumps anything that takes up a slot within it. Love, work, play, obligation, learning—these are not exclusive categories. However, the analytic (isolating, dualistic, oppositional) baskets in which we lump them in the medium of a neutralized measurement of time (as time itself) not only creates the illusion of a false separateness but keeps us on a treadmill of "life" that is constantly on or off deadline, but never running right.

There is no time for purpose. Purpose knows its own time and place, and while the frameworks into which we compartmentalize our lives would keep us marching on with or without enthusiasm, this is no substitute for true direction, natural interests and talents, expression and creativity, doing the work that isn't "work" in that it is loved so well. We have a barren stretch of mathematized time set aside for relaxation and we can't think of what to do with ourselves, certainly nothing novel, nothing inspiring. Why? Because the context we have overlooked has stung the content into a moribund state of paralysis. The context of the dialectical relations that inform have been torn from anything "natural" and turned over to clock time, arbitrary divisions, superficial distinctions, the yak-yak of what everyone "just knows." We have imposed a framework that freezes the dynamism of constitutive relations and that substitutes fragments for systems, parts for wholes, deadline drudgery for depth of experience. As Raymond Ku observed, even in Taiwan the lifestyle is fragmented. Fragmentation is the death knell for culture just as it is for language. Both only work as systems, given a certain unity.

My goal in this text is to inspire you to recommit to learning by thinking otherwise, by thinking more deeply and with more clarity, even on the subject of learning itself. A holistic and dialectical approach to thinking is here broached. This is a way of thinking that precludes the ossification of maps into irrelevance, a manner of thinking that at once sets the most advantageous course while leaving open the possibility of response, the agility to capitalize upon opportunity. Once this style of thought has been mastered, and this book is a prolonged exercise in its mastery, the learning process will take on a whole new significance, a freedom and ease that will permit you to understand complex systems and systems of systems much more readily in their underlying simplicity. You will be able to think about business and life more fruitfully, to engage with them more meaningfully and profitably, and to design systems or impose order in all areas of your life. Work and business are not tools in the service of life. If they were, they could be tossed aside like a pick and spade, and what would remain would be all of life. Work and business are continuous with life, of a piece with it.

In some ways, my life began in the meatpacking district of New York City, in the hours before dawn, with the rumble of the carts from the trucks and trains, carts loaded down with meat and dripping into the streets, the blood eventually covered over with sawdust. There was always a hollow footfall upon the rough cobblestones, the red and brown brick buildings that held the street as if within a cistern, producing the eerily mixed echoes of seagulls circling above and the clamor of men below. The separate smells of morning, last night's rain, old trash, fresh blood, half-congealed fat and sawdust all mingled together into a new smell, of which I grew quite fond as it became inseparable from the time and place, the people I knew then, the inauguration of a new idea, and something of a gamble.

The gamble undertaken involved a kid fresh out of college entering the Fourteenth Street Market of New York, a fading vestige of the Old World yet holding out against the encroachments of real estate developers, crack smokers peddling crime, cross-dressing prostitutes progressively waxing more and more aggressive. This was a place, with my early morning hours, where one could quite easily get hurt moving through the pre-dawn night in a double-breasted suit, not all that far from where the homeless children of the salt mountains of the West Side docks congregated to scour for scraps. The gamble was upon an idea, a new conception of networking. I had bucked "the system" to be here, and my career was on the line. I was living out the consequences of a decision I had made. I then learned that every moment is the moment of decision, and that the power of decision is much greater than most people imagine.

I am always struck anew by the deep complicity between the professional principles I hold most dear and the unfolding of my life as a whole, the details of my personal story. The ideas I have outgrown, even after years of conducting seminars for some of the biggest institutions in the world, despite the almost paternal satisfaction in long rosters of former students who have gone on to become industry-leading professionals—for just such feelings can all too often foster an attachment to views and methods in excess of the always accumulating evidence—were every bit as important as the much better grounded insights I would acquire downstream. The ability to hold a proposition open, even while one is acting upon it, is fundamental, and all of the propositions I held that changed and then were finally abandoned retained the power of having spoken to the time and of responding to the changing times. It is an achievement to stay abreast of the times, to recognize trends and stay ahead of them. And this requires the willingness, ultimately, to challenge some of our most cherished convictions. The conviction that cannot be challenged—because it becomes too closely identified with ourselves or too comforting or...or...-- becomes an albatross. Thinking ought to resemble a dance rather than a succession of frozen postures. But for thinking to dance there must be joy, and joy precisely in thinking. Consider the case of a salesperson fresh out of college. In the years prior to my teaching career, while searching for the kind of teaching position I wanted, I was a salesman.

If sales were a science, I could describe it and be done with it. I could show you how a^2 plus b^2 equals c^2 and the last word would have been said. This is a true proposition. In fact, it is the Pythagorean Theorem. It is eternally true. However, sales is neither pure science nor pure art; it is a hybrid discipline—all betwixt and between—and what is required to truly unleash your potential, to both succeed and enjoy your success (and the coincidence of these two phenomena cannot be emphasized sufficiently) is not only hard-won insights gained over years of dedication, insights which can be formulated as abstract principles (say, for the PowerPoint presentation with far more sleep-inducing power than the Sandman)--but a new way of thinking, new habits of thought. And with new ways of thinking comes the reconnection with and renewal of one's passion. The old thinking has stretched your passion to the breaking point, deprived you of a purpose with the power to be the engine of your life.

The only appropriate place to begin is with the first groundbreaking decision of my sales career, as a young man just out of college. I knew the risk I was taking, but I wasn't mature enough yet to trust fully my own intuition, the nearly inaudible whisper of something that seemed certain to the point of tautology. I attended to it, hesitated for a long while, made my decision—and have spent the rest of my life trying to explain to others what I knew then intuitively, to interpret the whisper. To a great extent, this is what my teaching and training have been, and this fact has forced me to retrace my steps a thousand times, but not only for myself. After a while, a teacher can only take himself seriously *vis-à-vis* his students, and the practice of teaching becomes inseparable from reflection, even if the object is one's own past. I was following my passion and engaged in a new way of thinking without even knowing it. It was exciting because I no longer followed the conventional wisdom. I was free. Adherence to the conventional wisdom is the opposite of being free; it is the avoidance of freedom, of making choices that really matter. One can never capitalize on opportunity while adhering to the conventional wisdom. If one thinks like the others, one makes the choices they make.

The specters of this early time in sales have been frequent visitors, even in my dreams, forming a great circle. Those I knew then were *my* teachers, presiding over the "self-whisperings" of a very young man, instructing him in the most concrete manner possible to trust both them and, with that, what he "overheard" in himself. I wasn't the center of this circle; I circulated through it, and now that it has marked me through and through, I see that it is also the circle by which those who have gone before keep the flame alight, the all-important passion, by making the evening years of their professional lives someone else's daybreak, by striking the flint of dusk for the spark of dawn. They too become mentors for those who have to begin thinking anew, starting with the most fundamental things of all, one's purpose. This is at the very center of the circle. It is what makes it possible. Chalkboard or iPad, the red-eye to Dallas or instant cyber-conferencing—the pace of change makes no difference here. What is true of purpose has always been true of it. We really must be careful not to allow ourselves to become the merest extensions of our instruments. We really must take care to never think of ourselves as high-end data processors. Purpose presupposes value, the existence of things qualitative. If anyone promises to map your brain and preserve your consciousness on a computer hard drive, run from this Dr. Frankenstein with all your might. Life without purpose is the merest jest, an empty nothing, and something considerably more than half the world is in the grip of this nothingness, this nihilism, this devaluation of all values, this sweeping cancellation of meaning.

The philosopher Plato traced the source of life in its eternal striving to Eros, which I will translate as passion (though *love* would be more literal). I was fortunate: I knew from the very first, day one of my career, that I had a passion for sales. I say that I was fortunate, for there are so many who do not have a passion, or who have had it and have lost it. They go on now, from day to day, for other reasons—for an income, the family, for the sake of staying busy or distracted, for retirement. Such a curious paradox, our view of retirement: to work for a lifetime so that one can finally stop working and full-throatedly proclaim "halleluiah" and "good riddance." It is a horrible spectacle if you allow yourself to linger with it, to make it the object of prolonged meditation. To contemplate being wide awake and quite active, going about one's daily life, and yet to be dead in *that* spot (of Eros), to be living out a routine, mechanical variations on the same stale theme. I don't know what Plato would say, but perhaps, if Eros or passion is the ground of life—always striving, always changing, doing, acting, thinking, meditating—those who have lost it...have died. So for the moment let's not wonder whether there is life after death. Let us wonder whether there is life prior to it. Anyone who could dream of life on a hard drive is closer to a potted plant than a human being, and in ways too numerous to mention the scientific infinite has become the presiding ideal, not merely in the West but the world over. Just think back on the kind of deference Raymond Ku expressed for the Western mind on precisely this score. It is great to have a menu to choose from, but not if there is no distinguishing the items that are poisonous. Isn't McDonald's, in its own way, poisonous?

Western science universalized is indeed a terrible thought. It suggests scenes in the cult classic *Texas Chainsaw Massacre*, the listless movement of zombies, their congregation in mute communities and around living victims who are to be devoured like chicken. I say in mute communities, hoping you will see this as something of a contradiction in terms. For linguistic beings, there is no silent community. But with all our technology, the silence is only growing. As MIT Professor Sherry Turkle recorded in her book *Alone Together*, "These days, insecure in our relationships and anxious about intimacy, we look to technology for ways to be in relationships and protect ourselves from them at the same time....We expect more from technology and less from each other." That is, the technology comes to do what we should be doing for ourselves, and inactivity stifles all creativity, all true engagement, purpose. It is easier to text bad news to a friend then be there face to face while she reels from it, and this avoidance quickly becomes a habit. We have today more friends than ever, and yet these friendships matter less than ever. We are more connected than ever, and less capable of reaching through to anyone. We have gone global in all manner of ways, and lack depth most profoundly. Our humanity is the thinnest imaginable gruel. Destroy community, as we have destroyed the natural world, and we lose all vitality. It is self-destruction by way of the other—an immensely important dialectic to grasp.

What is a community if one is alone in it, in the absence of interaction? Did you know that "more people live alone now than at any other time in history"? That is what the sociologist Eric Klinenberg claims. And yet we have never been alone. Not really. We have always been in community, situated among other people, thinking in and speaking the language by which we understand ourselves, the language that most emphatically belongs to others, even those long gone. But to truly be in it we must begin thinking for ourselves, stop allowing language and what others believe to think through us. The community that destroys creativity creates individuals who are only echoes of itself. It grows stagnant and creates only more stagnation. The same is true of an organization.

I recently had the author of the book *Friendfluence* on my radio program. Her name is Carlin Flora, one-time editor of *Psychology Today*, and she made the case that friendship could very well be a subject on the curriculum in our schools. This struck me as an interesting idea, but I am doubtful of its practicability. That is, our schools are trending so heavily in the direction of job training and career preparation, the idea of a course of immediate relevance to human beings but without any fiscal applicability seems little short of fantastic. I say this fully aware that such a course would indeed have "fiscal applicability," but the ability to see this is another matter. In that the conversation I had with Ms. Flora on the radio strikes directly to the heart of our concerns, I have reproduced a redacted version of the exchange here.

McCarty: I have a terrific guest on with me today. She's the author of *Friendfluence*. She was a writer and editor with *Psychology Today*. Her name is Carlin Flora. And the book's subtitle is *The Surprising Way Friends Make Us Who We Are*. You mention in your book a university professor who made the case that friendship should be a subject taught in the schools.

Carlin Flora: That is a wonderful psychologist who specializes in teenagers and adolescents. Friendship comes naturally to kids who are socially skilled, but not to a lot of other kids. They might be on the Asperger spectrum or shy. They might have trouble regulating their emotions. They might not be conscious of how much friends shape them going forward. Our thinking about friendship has become kind of passive. We wouldn't think teenagers would need to be taught.

McCarty: I am a critic of the school system. Since Horace Mann, more and more, our schools have been dedicated to training a workforce. Today we want to steer kids into subjects that will pay off down the road in job opportunities. Florida has proposed a tiered tuition system which would steer students into the hard sciences, software and computer design, etc. I wonder how much of this has to do with us taking the eye off the ball, neglecting the matters that should concern us most. What concerned me in high school, for instance, was the rather weird phenomenon by which I was (as cool, as valuable as) those with whom I associated. And then there was always the kid having lunch by himself, the kid who by now has probably incurred more psychotherapy bills than Woody Allen. The school, at that time and still today, seems so disengaged from all of this. I remember an administrator of Columbine High School, the site of the mass shootings, on television raising the question of how they (administrators) could possibly have known anything in advance. And all I could think of was how the gunmen—the gunboys, I guess—were long seen walking the hallways in trench coats while delivering "Heil Hitler" salutes to each other. It all seems fairly obvious, hard to miss. We all know who is getting excluded in high school. This isn't a secret. So are we going to use our schools to address issues of friendship and of our humanity or will we use them to subsidize corporate America, the companies that less and less invest in America?

Carlin Flora: Right. I think there are a lot of connections between what you are saying about retaining the humanities and studying friendship. One of the stats in my book which I found so surprising is that it only takes one friend to greatly decrease the chances of a child being bullied, and if she is bullied, to greatly decrease the chance of her developing depression as a result. So with all the media attention on bullying, I think we need to do that. We need an anti-bullying program, but I think a nice complement, for something with broader appeal, would be a pro-friends program. Not just anti-bully, but raising the question, What are the values of friendship? How can we be a good friend? We could start from that positive place rather than demonize the bully.

McCarty: I like the title, *Friendfluence*. What do you think about the claim so many people are making today, the claim that people spend more time alone than ever, that in America friendship isn't valued all that much, that friends have become disposable?

Flora: I think that's a little harsh. I think Americans do value friendship a lot. We value independence because we are less enmeshed in family structure than some other cultures. But this can make us even more attached to friends. But I see your bigger point. I think it is true that we don't strive to be *great* friends, that maybe this kind of friendship is not a value of our culture, even if friends are important to us because of our relative independence. If you think about this in terms of evolution, of how humans developed historically, we're in these small groups. And it was extremely important for us to stay in with that small group and not get expelled from it, or we would literally die. So I think when you remember that, it reinforces the importance psychologically of fitting into the classroom for the child, and why, as you're saying, a teacher should be attuned to that little tribe. What's going on there, who is feeling excluded, who is trying to gain power in an aggressive way, etc?

McCarty: You mention in your book an evolutionary psychologist who theorizes that friendship has its roots in early human interdependence for purposes of survival. Evolutionary theory seems to present an enormous canvas for speculation, perhaps even loose and jazz-improvisational thinking.

Flora: Right. Evolutionary psychology does a good job explaining feelings and drives that are difficult to comprehend rationally. It doesn't mean that we shouldn't try to master or overcome them or that culture does not play a role. But it does a good job of explaining why fitting into a group is so important, why being excluded hurts so much. But that does not mean that we should stop there. Evolutionary psychology is just a starting point, a window on human nature, and from there you can go on to talk about what we are discussing, friendship skills, overcoming the need to aggressively assert oneself in a hierarchy.

McCarty: You address in your book the perception of a generational shift. You say that friends have taken on a different value given trends of the last 30 years or so. You mention young adults living at home with their parents, retarding maturation.

Flora: I did not suggest a retardation of maturation in the sense of a value judgment. Friends are more important because of demographic factors. We are marrying later or not at all. I don't consider that immature. It is what it is. A lot of people are not enmeshed in extended families. There are more only children than there used to be. All these factors coming together result in people living alone, whether they are widowed, divorced, or single. And that means that friends are fulfilling roles that family members used to fulfill.

McCarty: You're right. You didn't say that. That was me unfairly reading between the lines. I do have to wonder at the enormous complexity of friendship. It isn't just a question of sharing the same values. It seems like there is a reason why, when people come to talk about intimacy, they fall into the vague terminology of "chemistry" or whatever. We didn't "click."

Flora: Right. Friendship is hard to define. It is flexible. It could be with someone you just "clicked" with. It can be a connection, a feeling that someone really gets you and understands. The research shows that sometimes it's like that, and our friends are people quite similar to ourselves. But research also shows that friendships with people who are different from you can be really satisfying. That's a good reminder to people to sometimes go against the natural tendency when making friends.

McCarty: On the one hand, being a friend means that you observe certain norms or, if you violate them, that you do it with finesse. You mention in your book a very charismatic woman who was kind of a smash, really terrific, but ended up a stripper and a drug user. Here you have someone who treads the fine line between groupthink and autonomy. It doesn't seem like a simple line to draw. If you don't think for yourself, you aren't actually free. You're just plugged into the group mind. So the trick is to think for yourself without becoming a weirdo.

Flora: I actually doubt the whole concept of thinking for yourself, because we are so influenced by other people. We are so attuned to the norms of the group. If we violate the norms consciously we have the need to connect to people who are doing that too. This is misfits banding together. So I think even people who fancy themselves to have a very individual way of thinking, that they too are allied to a group, even if it is a group outside the mainstream.

McCarty: You addressed Picasso and Matisse in the book. Picasso was a genius and deeply strange. He meets Matisse and they become friends. Picasso ends up doing in sheet metal what Matisse did in paper.

Flora: Right. Each recognized the genius in the other. Each thought of the other as on his own level. That was their connection. "I finally found another genius."

McCarty: I wanted to ask about the title of your book, *Friendfluence*. I have been reading about mirror cells in the brain. So, for instance, a woman born without arms and legs is exposed to images of people eating apples, knitting, jogging, and so forth. And it turns out that the exact same brain activity transpires in the watching woman—the activity of eating, knitting, jogging. It's as if she were doing it herself.

Flora: Right. And it's the same if we watch sports and other activities.

McCarty: Someone like Hegel or Jacques Lacan is not going to describe this in terms of brain chemistry. They are going to say that we learned who we were in a kind of mirror. They will say that there is a mirroring that takes place. I wonder if the idea of influence between people seems more mysterious than it actually is. And maybe it seems mysterious because we all share a fundamental misconception of the self as a sort of isolated thing, a soul atom, rather than a collective thing. Some people think of the self as a narrative. This, of course, offends our individualism to the foundation. But what if we are not the isolated atoms we think? What if we are the products of language, of history?

McCarty: Right. I think you are absolutely right. It's a bias we have. We think that the self is a closed off, finite personality, that I make my own choices, exercise free will. We operate under these assumptions. Then when you look at it from the outside, you see that we're just constantly influenced by our social environment, in both small and large ways. We want to connect on the level of the personality, but there's usually a combination of qualities and people around them who are influencing them. Or there is a lack of people around them in the case of loneliness, and what this does to your mental and biological health.

McCarty: I think too of the Greek chorus. The Greek chorus was something like the voice of the community. It spoke for the audience. Well, our Greek chorus today is the laugh track. The TV laughs for us. I have seen people watch TV and their faces are just flat, unchanging. You ask them how the show was, and they say it was hysterical. It looks like the TV is doing the laughing for them. In a similar connection, I am thinking of the Kardashians and why people are watching other people getting along or not getting along. Why sit and watch ordinary human relationships rather than have them oneself?

Flora: I have heard psychologists say that deep down we think of these people as our friends. It feels like they are in our social circle. That's why we have this hunger for gossip about celebrities. The more we know about them, the more we are drawn in. It is also a way to project our fears or anxieties about social interaction, watching shows that feature fighting and that thrive on conflict. I think women in particular will watch. A lot of women have a fear of conflict.

McCarty: You mentioned in the book that you as a girl had imaginary friends, and that they even fought with each other.

Flora: I mentioned that as an aside, that I had two grown men for imaginary friends. It is common for kids to have them. It points to something vital in our development, that kids are working out how to be a friend even before they have a real one. And there are cognitive parallels. Imaginary friends teach us how to take another's perspective, how to argue, how to consider another's idea and evaluate it, to compare your own notions with theirs. And you can use your friends' knowledge of you to change yourself for the better, which I think might be the highest benefit of friendship. A lot of people do not like their friends to ever criticize or question them. In my book, I try to make it clear that the best kind of friend is supportive but will occasionally give you some difficult feedback. The friend knows you so well that she can help you grow.

McCarty: Interpersonal negotiation is like learning to dance with someone perhaps. You not only learned from your imaginary friends, you went beyond that. You identified with them. This wasn't some kind of causal relationship. However, it seems to me that reality is, in great part, resistance. I know that my kids have grown up with more technology than I did, certainly. They are not as comfortable with the natural world as people have been. Nature is not air-conditioned, it doesn't deposit ice into a cup. My concern is that the virtual world, the virtual classroom, the virtual friendship, the delayed departure from home is going to cost people in self-worth, the self-worth of enjoying the resistance. Maybe some people never get to that point, the enjoyment of anxiety.

Flora: I think that is a profound worry given how much kids are into devices. But there is no reason to panic. Kids are still developing social lives even in the real world, even if they are concurrently developing them online. Yeah, you definitely need time with people face to face to develop empathy skills.

McCarty: You cited a sociologist who says that more people live alone now than in any time in history. But you are suggesting that this is not because they are without friends.

Flora: Right. Quite the contrary. The research is that people who live alone socialize more. This makes sense. When people get married, especially if they have jobs and kids, the friends are relegated to the bottom of the list. A lot of people who live alone in fact have richer friendships and better social lives than people who live with others. It's a lesson for married people, to remember to nurture their friendships, which in turn help their romantic lives. Loneliness is metaphorically tantamount to death. If you are completely checked out of your group, your tribe, you are left to die.

****

I always wonder, upon placing myself on a dais before an auditorium of strangers, an audience expecting me to knock something out quickly, like a horseshoe from a practiced blacksmith, all in a rapid-fire series of blows, how I should begin, whether my listeners will have the patience to take a step or two toward a new way of thinking. I can't just say outright, like an Old Testament prophet, that we have lost our passion, our Eros, that we move among the dead. Who am I to say such a thing? It might be true, but I cannot say it. You will have to listen to yourselves, overhear your own self-whisperings, look about you and decide. This is the kind of learning that one must ultimately do for oneself. It is without truth otherwise. It cannot be received as a set of declarations in the form of X is Y.

I also cannot command my audience to take note, to observe that we have already wandered into the province of the "betwixt and between." We have considered the living dead, the mute community, the social being that now prefers being alone, the claim that outgrown or refuted ideas remain instructive, that the way to participate in community is first to distinguish oneself from it. Have we not covered a most paradoxical ground? This might be true, but I cannot say it. The audience would think me joking, would suspect me of quibbling, of wasting their time.

So I tend to begin with a story, one that makes the point— the exact same—without saying it: We do move among the walking dead and that is largely because of an unwillingness to abide being "betwixt and between." We want certainty without realizing that those who live the somnambulist's life are not principally troubled by uncertainty. In fact, they have taken extreme measures to insure that not the slightest hint of it ever arises, by becoming the creatures of a thoroughgoing routinization. That is to say that they have lost the passion, that they have set out on a routine, have made this decision, consciously or unconsciously, and that the routine now decides, calls the shots for them. And that would mean that even routine, even repetition (as Kierkegaard observed) is betwixt and between. It is the decision to progressively deprive oneself of the responsibility and stress of decision-making, the decision that rejects all decision making, that in the moment of decision rejects decisiveness with contempt. The thoughtless habit (or habit of thought) makes decision impossible. Repetition forecloses the possibility of decision, and a false sense of security envelops all. If the captain piloting our plane were in this condition, there would be reason to reach for our flotation devices.

How awake are you? Do you hear me right now? If not, what is stopping you? The same whisperings that will reveal the truth to you of how you stand with Eros can also disclose the extent to which your life, personal and professional, has become weighed down with routine. If it isn't, you should be quite light on your feet. You shouldn't require the high-octane of a Starbucks "grande" to power you through the day.

I have already mentioned a decision I made as a young man. I have spoken of it as a gamble, a risk. The English poet and literary critic Matthew Arnold mentioned the need to cherry-coat medicine so that our children will swallow it. But there is no cherry-coating the truth that decisions of consequence, given that none of us is omniscient, contain an ineffaceable element of risk and that risk is inherently stressful, and I don't know what to do for a child who just won't take his medicine, no matter how it is lacquered in artificial flavors.

Aristotle, the great philosopher, observed that man is not meant to live alone, that the one who lives alone is either a beast or a god—or, perhaps, as we tend to think today, an egomaniacal mass murderer in the making. I tend not to share Carlin Flora's rather optimistic view of how things stand with us in the West as social beings. The trend that I see toward social unfitness might not result in an epidemic of mass murder—in our schools or inner cities—but it would say something about our individual prospects of a decent quality of life. In this regard, there was a study of nurses afflicted with breast cancer. It was found that those without a close friend died at 400% the rate of those with one or more. The mortal body knows the difference, but what it knows can only be whispered. And those who whisper risk going unheard, entertaining listeners who aren't in fact listening. Those who aren't listening: perhaps the "friends" on Facebook. No one has to tolerate a hard truth there. There is no place better prepared for the lifelong practice of avoidance than cyberspace. It isn't, as Ms. Flora maintains, that people today maintain friends online and offline. The hard work of friendship had shifted, and Americans have never found themselves as socially incompetent as they are today. And this social incompetence feeds into a much wider phenomenon, systems collapse. There is the failure of our schools, of our government, of our economy. Even our guiding notions of how business ought to be done are backward.

My message for business people cannot be reduced to the Pythagorean Theorem. The theorem leaves no room for doubt, no space for decision, for the moment of risk, the willingness to listen to a whisper and leap into the darkness—the darkness which might turn out to be a light so bright it is too much for our unaccustomed eyes, the mere appearance of darkness. Instead I will proceed in my own way, with a paradox: Human beings are the social creatures who only attain dignity (or any other great height or achievement) in their autonomy. Autonomy is only possible for a people released into their own creativity, and the hard sciences we are urged—bribed, in fact—to study are only making us stupid.

This is the self-contradictory principle from which I start. I take a risk and choose a beginning in the middle, with a gamble I made as a young adult. I don't mention my nativity, this beginning. And there are likely to be critics, strange ones, who would like me to start at the end. They would like me to share "the secrets" I have stored up over the years, that have ripened only now, in the autumn of my career. I have no choice. I must engage these critics, albeit hypothetical, immediately. The ever-pressing demand to "Get to the point" is the suppression of all thinking, ostensibly out of the belief that there is only *thinking*—one word, one kind of activity. And, further, that we know what it is. But the truth is something else again. What if thinking is not either-or, this or that? What if thinking is all betwixt and between, dialectical, relational, holistic? What then?

Why would one want me to start at the end? Would you like to be where I am now, approaching the end of a career and retirement? Has the cultural pandemic of ADHD spread so far, reached so deep, that we are in so much of a hurry to get to the end, wanting it from the very start, that nothing can induce us to linger? No need to sweat the track when you go directly from start to the finish line. Is the Eros supporting your striving only the wish for security, which can only happen if everything is over, if success has been won in advance...of being achieved, of all of the striving that makes it possible? Your Eros then would be the striving that came to be called *Thanatos* or the death drive, the striving intent upon ending all striving. The striving that Plato attributes fundamentally to life, in such a case, would be obsessed with death, the complete cessation of striving (or Eros). It would be the passion for the achievement of the state of passionlessness. Perhaps the zombie of our cinematic imagination is caught in this circle. He is alive only in the sense that he loves death, identifies with it, has a passion for it. The dead take no risks, make no decisions, face no uncertainty, and the passionless routinization of all things is zomboid.

My question was, Why would you have me start at the end, make a beginning there? I remind you of this question not because you are in need of reminder, but because it is always possible that there are those who are listening without being awake. My audience is in the position of the listener. I am in that of the teacher. If either of us stops doing what we ought, at that very moment, we will no longer be what we were—me teaching (as a teacher ought) and you listening (as a member of an audience ought). And yet many of you have decided already what I ought to do, namely begin at the end. My role as teacher has been usurped, for it is now the student who decides for me, who already knows about teaching and how it ought to proceed, and how am I or anyone else to teach such a student anything? He already knows, or thinks he does. He insists that I begin at the end and have done with it. This is the dialectical relation we occupy with respect to each other. So if we are to begin to learn (for the first time), we must unlearn a great deal. Let's set about this at once.

Imagine my subject is sales. Do you have a passion for it? Pythagoras cannot answer this question for you. You have to look, assume the autonomy by which you determine how things stand with yourself. Such direct looking must be the product of autonomy; it is not possible for anyone to do it for you. Your business is sales, and where would you be if you discovered here and now or someplace else sometime that you don't care for it all that much, that you lack passion for it? One might think this a great catastrophe, but I don't see it that way. Could it ever really be too late to learn what one really ought to be doing? Would it be better to never come into the knowledge at all? Would it be better to learn it at the end of a career, that you have been unhappy doing what you have done all your life? And what is this life you haven't exactly chosen? Who has chosen it for you, and why did you let this other choose it?

If you were one of those who wanted me to begin at the end, to say in a lucid set of assertions what I have learned about sales, concisely share my so-called wisdom, so as to give you a leg up—to you only I ask, Why? For every movie on the market today, hundreds and hundreds of them, I can tell you in a succinct phrase how they end, one and all. If one ought to begin at the end, I can do it, obey the student's instructions on instruction, the student's dictates to the teacher. I can go beyond prediction, say with Pythagorean certainty how every film on the market the world over ends.

But would you want me to tell you? Perhaps not. You have a passion for movies. Were I to give away the ending, you would be deprived of what passion wants most, to linger. This is a proposition. Put it to the test. Consider whether your spouse or children would like you to linger with them a bit. Reply "no" and I am forced to respond: If so, they are not human. Perhaps they are gods or beasts? It would seem that to be human is to be betwixt and between—that is, relative to gods and beasts. To linger passionately is, as such, human. To linger: to stay a while, to pause on the way, to be underway, to be betwixt and between. And only a holistic-dialectical approach can speak to lingering, to the state of being betwixt and between.

But I have decided. I will take the risk of your displeasure and tell you the ending of every movie on the screens of all of the theaters in the world today. I will risk incurring your disapproval by shattering all chance of lingering with the film about which you are passionate. I will do it in a single phrase, so that the beginning may be such that we reach the end all in a stroke, without all of the striving otherwise required: Credits roll. *Exeunt omnes*.

The desire for this, the hurry to reach the end, is *Thanatos* (the death drive)-- not *Eros*.

It turns out that my answer is correct (or, at the very least, highly probable, true in the main), but also that I haven't given anything away. I do not stand between you and your passionate lingering, your desire to be in the midst of something, underway to someplace great but not yet arrived. I stand *between*, but not between you and your Eros. I facilitate your striving, which as an audience you ought to have. It isn't as if there could be a substitute for it, and a substitute can't find it for you. By now, at some level of consciousness, you know whether your purpose is of the kind that sustains. There is no need to wait. You know it now. And it could be that the *way you strive, the manner of your striving*, reflects the nature or condition of your purpose.

You strive to take something of value from what I am presenting in my capacity as one who knows, and the striving ceases once you have attained your goal. We move from an imagined stasis to another position, also static. If Eros is life or striving or passion or preference—whatever word you like—the achievement of the ultimate goal is to die--credits roll, nothing more of interest, *exeunt omnes*. But in standing between, I would ask you to linger—to stay a while with what is passing, on its way, short of its goal, yet inspired with passion. I would start with the beginning, as it concerns us here and now, and that is the question of your passion. It is also the question of autonomy for a social or non-autonomous being. Only you can "look" and decide: Do you have a passion for sales? Does sales get you out of the bed in the morning like a missile? Are you ready to give up on the conventional wisdom, on what "just everyone" knows?

Larry King, the famous broadcaster and CNN interviewer, was once asked how he could return to the mike after all the years he had passed before one. His response was eloquent in its brevity. He said, "It is the only thing I would miss breakfast to do." What would you miss breakfast for, and miss it often (in defiance of your dietician)? Even if the wolves were not at the door, if you had achieved some comfort in life—if you were no longer living from check to check, no longer unsure of whether you would "make it"—would you skip breakfast to make a sales call? Now, I think, here in the middle, we have (once again) arrived at the beginning. It might very well depend upon *the kind of sales call you are to make*. It will depend upon what the sales call *means*, whether this significance is wide and deep or the opposite.

The taproot of all progress is purpose, and we need very desperately to know more about it. It is with purpose, at this point of origin, that the personal and the professional reveal themselves most obviously as one and the same. A purpose, to be sustained, must set a course that is quite definite but leave open sufficient opportunity for changed circumstances. So students who think that their college degree will simply translate into "some kind of job" are less likely to earn it than those who want to be teachers and are studying education, than those who want to be accountants and are studying accounting, and so on. A sustained purpose depends upon the clarity with which the goal is conceived in its possibility. It is not merely a matter of feeling, but of thinking, and the recognition that thinking and feeling are by no means contraries.

For the archer, there are infinite ways to miss the bull's eye and only one path to hitting it. But when there is no bull's eye at all, the man armed with the bow is not an archer. He is a danger to himself and others, a menace. The goal (the bull's eye) sustains him in his character as an archer, and most college students can't answer a simple question, "What is the highest value in your life? What is the one thing you want above all others?" To ask this is to ask, what's the bull's eye? Does your life have an overarching goal? If it does not, there will be no satisfying economy of movement. Life will be a frustrating, rudderless maze of wrong, time-wasting turns. One will change majors over and over and never graduate.

The purpose and the goal are inseparable. No goal, no purpose. No purpose, no goal. They are dialectically related, mutually constituting.

The purposeless life is not an ideal of some sort. It is inertia of a kind so pure that human endeavor is unsustainable. We need at least the purpose of taking care of ourselves to some degree, and we need a great deal more than that for a flourishing and satisfying life. We are only deficient in "will power" if we lack purpose, clarity in our goals. The answer to deficient will power is not bucking up, whatever that means, but thinking differently.

We need to consider the dependence of purpose upon the goal carefully. In the case of the college student, as in most other cases, the goal must be of a certain clarity and degree of attainability for purpose to endure. The hazy goal of "some kind of job" sustains purpose as poorly as the nearly unattainable one of "President of the United States." Everyone knows of Bill Clinton and his early cultivation of this goal, of becoming President. Everyone has heard a parent say, "You can be anything you want when you grow up, even President of the United States." The problem with this presumably optimism-inspiring, liberating claim is that it is false, and we don't want to be liberated into fantasy. The problem with the Bill Clinton example is that it is a classic instance of the logical fallacy of hasty generalization. I know someone who once one the lottery, but that does not increase my odds of winning it. The odds remain for me the same as those of being struck by lightning. That Bill Clinton became President doesn't affect *your odds* in this regard in the least. Our thinking is infused with all manner of myths and fallacies. We speak, for instance, of being on a "hot streak." But the circumstance that one has thrown double-sixes four times in a row has nothing whatever to do with the odds of throwing them a fifth time.

What then will serve as our guide in thinking through the relationship of purpose to goal? It will be a method of learning. We must learn about ourselves to arrive at a suitable purpose sustained by a realistic goal. I must in fact possess musical talent to aspire to be a professional musician. I must know what I can do before I can know what I should do. Again, it just isn't true that we can be anything at all—sumo wrestler or priest, painter or prophet, mathematician or tango master. And this is a good thing. We can only make something of our lives if our plans are reality-based, both in terms of who we are and in terms of what we actually accomplish. The famous McDonald's brothers, Maurice and Dick, decided in 1948 that they were bored with the hamburger business, that it provided insufficient purpose, and McDonald's became the concern of someone else.

We must then begin with self-understanding and our commitment to achieve more of it. Our commitment must be as strong as if life itself hung in the balance. And it does. We have to be convinced that the unexamined life is not worth living, and that means turning our attention to what is nearest at hand—to ourselves. We are hardest to see because we are so near. We don't look to the lenses of our glasses but to the objects of the world. However, we should look near, if only because what we will be looking at won't be anything like as uninteresting as lenses, the transparent "nothing" through which we see. We will be looking literally at how our whole world, our experience, gets constructed, takes on meaning or loses it, assumes vibrancy or pales away into humdrum routine. Our purpose will not only provide the motivation we require; it will enable us to perceive opportunity. We must have a purpose to identify that which will serve our purpose. A new way of thinking provides us with new optics, with fresh eyes.

A business organization, like the individual person, is set into motion on the basis of a *purpose*. A purpose is the pre-actualized conception of what needs to be done. A business sets out with the purpose of making money. An individual person is guided in his or her affairs by a purpose—to stay alive, to remain healthy, to achieve happiness, to find love and belonging. In both cases, a single purpose is insufficient. In other words, purposes must be multiple and they must stand to each other in hierarchical order. Our approach must be holistic for this reason: There are no self-sustaining, isolated purposes. They are necessarily multiple and in need of order.

Traditional analysis reduces everything to atoms and external relations among them. Dialectical analysis traces the constitutive relationships that make a holistic view meaningful. The traditional and the holistic-dialectical—these are two ways of thinking with radically different ramifications.

The business that sets out with the purpose of making money is in the earliest stage of formation. It exists only as an abstraction, though a necessary one. The purpose of making money must find warrant, justification, tools of assessment *in additional purposes*. So, for example, a business could make the determination that it will manufacture textiles, and the two purposes for which the business entity exists can be expressed succinctly: It exists to make a profit in the production of textiles. To this pair of purposes, a third must be added. It must be decided *where* production facilities are to be built, where the most appropriate supplies of labor are to be accessed, what is the proper mix of automations and human labor, and innumerable other matters. Each determination yields a purpose, and it is already possible to see that motivating purposes necessarily fall into a hierarchy. At its most fundamental, an actionable plan is a hierarchy of purposes, purpose organized. Everything else is incoherence.

Imagine that Acme Company owns a facility that contains industrial sewing machines. The company exists to make a profit by sewing pieces of fabric into shirts and dresses, which are then sold by another company, a retailer. However, war is declared and the domestic economy is mobilized for the manufacture of military supplies. The owners of Acme are presented with a choice. They can accept the price the government offers for the entire company and sell the business, or they can convert the manufacturing facility to the production of uniforms for the various branches of the armed forces.

Putting aside for the moment considerations of nationalism, ideology, perceptions of justified or unjustified military adventures and so on, Acme will stay true to its highest (and most abstract) purpose, the making of a profit. This was of course its principal reason for existence. For the owners of Acme, the question now becomes one of whether there is more possibility for profit (or for minimization of loss) in the sale of the company or in its continued operation under government terms as a supplier of uniforms. The company can be given up entirely, with all of its other (lower) purposes, to procure a sum that is larger than might otherwise be obtainable, whether in the short or long term, through continued operation. However, if the return realizable by way of continued operation, though with respect to a new purpose (i.e., the production of military uniforms), outweighs the sum offered in sale of the company, the highest purpose of the business entity is best served in wartime conversion.

Each purpose must be weighed, and weighed not only in terms of its own feasibility but also according to its hierarchical consistency (i.e., the determination of whether it is consistent with other organizational purposes). Until a purpose has been clearly articulated and all of its constitutive elements defined, it receives a red light. After it has been clearly articulated and while it is being subjected to evaluation, the light is yellow. When a clearly articulated and defined proposition or expression of the proposed purpose passes through the most rigorous evaluation and emerges, either in the original or in a revised form, the light goes to green. However, a green light at this point is nothing like license for squealing tires and rubber-burning smoke. It is but the beginning of a process replete with refinements and safeguards.

A mental model refers to the cognitive processes that are invoked and applied to the purpose that has been clearly formulated as a proposition or declarative sentence. The model can rely upon a quantitative, qualitative, or a hybrid approach. However, no matter what the approach, every model rests foundationally upon assumptions that give rise to conscious belief. And the most effective models are recursive, including as a structural feature the redundancy that acts as a failsafe. The redundancy keeps the orienting proposition open while testing it through all modification for continued accuracy. This is the crucial paradox, to go forward on the basis of a proposition that is kept open.

In the case of Acme Company, the purpose that would be realized in the production of shirts and dresses has to be formulated clearly. A clear formulation of the purpose might look like this proposition: Acme Company will employ its industrial sewing machines to assemble the fabrics of YIP shirts and VIP dresses. When this proposition is subjected to the mental model, to our model of rational decision-making, all manner of assumptions and beliefs will be unearthed, and new or revised purposes generated. However, the first step in the application of the mental model is to *convert* the proposition at issue into a hypothesis (without any loss of clarity). Our hypothesis might now look like this: Acme Company, by employing its industrial sewing machines to assemble the fabrics of YIP shirts and VIP dresses, will compete successfully with all extant or anticipated competitors.

The formulation of the guiding purpose as a proposition is critical. It is best to formulate and reformulate this proposition until all possible ambiguity is rung out of it, until it is as a declarative statement what a line is in geometry (the regulatory ideal in economy, the shortest distance between two points). However, there is no "hard science" to assist in the achievement of absolute succinctness. The approach that must be taken is qualitative (hermeneutical or interpretive). But let's say that the reading of the initial proposition lacks rigor, that an ambiguity somehow slips through, eludes the detection of all testing. The conversion of the purpose-proposition into a hypothesis acts as a failsafe measure. It now becomes highly likely that the initial ambiguity will be detected. Indeed, the more an idea or set of ideas is rephrased or rephrased and converted toward a different immediate end, the more the merely linguistic "surface" lifts from the ideational core. Only given the possibility of this "lifting" is it possible to tell whether the language expresses precisely the purpose or idea intended. And if the purpose is unclear, the goal will be as well.

Language all too often stands between us and the authenticity of purpose. If we speak in too loose a way about what we want, it is easy to go astray, to mislead ourselves into believing that we are following our passion when in fact we are conforming, living up to other people's ideas of what is best. We then find ourselves getting stuck. Something very like this happened to Dick and Maurice McDonald, the famous McDonald's brothers, in the late 1940s. They thought they were following their passion only to discover, all in an instant (as if they had been sleepwalking), that they no longer wanted to continue doing what they had done so well. They lost sight of what they wanted in the habit of actualizing every day what they always had wanted. One might say that they had become zomboid. What is wonderful about a proposition is that it can be preserved and retained in consciousness. It acts as a check upon the loss of wakefulness.

As such, the formulation of the purpose into a proposition is not a mere exercise. It is an indispensable means by which the reality of what is being conceived is placed into high relief and retained. In that the approach taken is necessarily qualitative (dealing in motivation, desire, pleasure, passion), it isn't foolproof. However, the approach rises to the very highest standard of reliability given sufficient structural redundancy. That is, the initial formulation is reformulated or converted into a hypothesis, and any inadequacy that escaped notice upon initial testing is now quite likely to show itself. The movement from formulation to reformulation, this redundancy, creates levels of reliability that meet and transcend the data quantitatively derived. The initial proposition undergoes continually reiteration and occasional modification, and this retention in repetition is the key to the achievement of actionable knowledge that permits agility, that wards off the dangers of routinization. Attend further to the example we have been considering.

A proposition (Acme Company will employ its industrial sewing machines to assemble the fabrics of YIP shirts and VIP dresses) has been converted into a hypothesis (Acme Company, by employing its industrial sewing machines to assemble the fabrics of YIP shirts and VIP dresses, will compete successfully with all extant or anticipated competitors). An ambiguity does emerge, but not one that was contained in the proposition. Precisely what is meant by *successful competition* must be spelled out. One's assumption might be that we are all big boys and girls and that, as such, we know quite well what we mean by the phrase. However, as we shall see, no assumption is more deceptive. The goal of analysis is not the compounding of complexity. It is simplification. A good analyst is never "above" reduction of any given thing, phenomenon, event, or system to its simplest elements. In fact, such reduction is the whole point. We can't afford to engage in loose talk.

Those who would found Acme Company gather around a table and raise the question of what would constitute successful competition, and they discover that at this level of abstraction or generality the question has no answer. They must know who their competitors are, where they are operating, and at what cost, with what profit margins and so on. If there is widespread flight of textile-producing capital from China, let's say, arriving at the cause(s) for it is crucial. Naturally, it is possible to pursue a quantitative course, to conduct a survey of those who have relocated a textile plant from China to another country (e.g. Bangladesh, Mexico, the USA) or to consult the findings of a survey that has been done independently. But it could also be that the prospective founders of Acme will have to again take a qualitative approach. That is, they will have to consult the data with respect to China and perform the closest possible reading. It could be, for instance, that there is no evidence of a backlash in, say, the United States against the production of these textiles (shirts and dresses of this kind) in China, but that the median wage of the workers who operate the industrial sewing machines has climbed high enough that profit margins have been squeezed. This effect when combined with the additional transportation costs from Asia to the US has resulted, we shall say, in a significant transfer of production facilities to the United States. Let's briefly review what has been achieved thus far, quite early in the decision-making process, by Acme Company.

Acme assumes that even if not the "end of history," capitalism is such that business opportunities remain, even within the contentious textile industry. Hence they believe it possible to profit by way of founding a business and, contrary to the beliefs of a great many American companies, achieve the best return on its investment via textile manufacturing. Acme assumes further that the only proper way to make an investment (rather than place a gamble) is on the basis of as complete a knowledge of the marketplace as possible. The company then acts on the assumption by conducting an analysis of textile manufacturing the world over. All of this might sound too painfully obvious to merit mention. But the reality is that the kind of learning and knowledge acquisition depicted above is so natural, so thoroughly logical, because it does indeed tap into how we learn best, most easily, most deeply. In a moment, the principles of learning that yield what seems like common sense now will remain fully in force as we move through tangled thickets of globalized complexity, as complexity is piled upon complexity.

We move from the proposition that Acme Company will employ its industrial sewing machines to assemble the fabrics of YIP shirts and VIP dresses to the hypothesis that Acme will thereby compete successfully with all extant or anticipated competitors. The hypothesis was then tested against a careful reading of the data. The inference was drawn that the kind of manufacturing Acme seeks to undertake can be most profitably pursued in the United States. In other words, we have moved from the initial proposition to a hypothesis that upon analysis has yielded yet another hypothesis. However, nothing has been lost. The proposition with which we began has been retained through two rather different hypotheses. As such, any ostensible drawback that might attend non-quantitative approaches (hermeneutical or phenomenological) is overcome by way of the structural redundancy that permits the retention of fundamental contents (the first proposition and the first hypothesis in the second hypothesis). Fundamental contents remain available and open for repeated testing, for the accumulation of much larger amounts of data, and the greatest danger in such a proceeding, premature closure, is avoided. The "argument" remains open as long as possible, deferring the fateful conclusion until the best possible case, the highest grade of validity, can be achieved. When the time comes to invoke fate, as it always does, no degree of certainty is superfluous. In this way, qualitative approaches produce the certainty typically associated with quantitative. Regardless of the dictates of conventional wisdom, for which this claim is anathema, it can be demonstrated quite easily.

Several kinds of *external constraints* have entered into the deliberations of Acme. *Current constraints* are expenses, and in this category the Acme entrepreneurs determined the cost of labor, overhead, transportation (among others) in the US as compared to elsewhere in the world. Acme found that total expense would be lowest in the United States, and by a significant margin. *Future constraints* or risks were also accounted for to the extent possible. There has been over the last 12 months an uptick in the demand for US-made textiles given the domestic fear and loathing of Chinese manufacturing generally and the massively damaging bad press coming out of Bangladesh. Companies too are responding. They are looking for higher quality products, delivered more reliability, and without the liability exposure and brand-stigmatizing fallout from oversees outsourcing. This suggests a trend that works toward the reduction of risk vis-à-vis Acme, though it is a trend that requires careful analysis to elucidate. The identification of a trend is the prerequisite to opportunity, the only means of getting out ahead of it.

In the last 23 years, 77% of the work force in the American textile and apparel industries has been lost due to companies relocating overseas. As such, the question that arises is whether the supply of laborers with the right skills remains abundant or can quickly be cultivated. The cut-and-sew jobs that Acme is contemplating are plagued by labor shortages. The owners of Acme know that the rapidly rising wages for these jobs (13.2% in the period from 2007 to 2012) are the direct result of insufficient supply, of companies having to pay more to attract more workers. (During the same period, 2007 to 2012, wages in the private sector grew just 1.4 %.) The question for Acme then is whether enough momentum exists--in the form of capital investment, state and federal incentives, regulatory frameworks, cultural norms, political commitments and so on—to address the labor shortage with sufficient rapidity to forestall the evaporation of cost advantages.

There are also *internal constraints* to be factored in. The *current constrains* include the amounts of investment capital the founders of Acme have at their disposal, the expenditure in time and energy that must be made in the present and so on. The *future constraints* have to do with long-term considerations, such as the infrastructural agility of Acme to respond quickly to new opportunities, the need to maintain brand integrity while adapting to the stresses of hypermobility and technological change, etc. And here is the critical point: This can only occur if the motivating propositions remain available and are in fact open to ongoing interrogation. Only ongoing interrogation (or what in one of its aspects I have called redundancy) can enable the company to respond appropriately to *what is not yet*, the future.

Constraints, whether internal or external, always must be considered ultimately in terms of the future. The level of one's unavoidable costs at the present moment draws its full consequence tomorrow or the day after, sometime in the future. And a model for rational decision making is useless without a robust capacity for the analysis of uncertainty, of that which is not yet. With respect to this crucial dimension of analysis there can never obtain the iron-clad certainty of 3 times 7 equals 21. However, data can be processed in such a way that uncertainty is decreased as much as possible, and in this regard every model for rational deliberation is not equal to every other. A successful model should be a means to the collection of the right information for the articulation of the clearest goals possible and the ongoing testing of precepts by which standards are validity are continually climbing. The proposition that is bundled in a hierarchy and that survives retention enables one to think about the future in the most exact and "scientific" manner possible. The future is not inherently a blank field for conjecture, but not everyone is equally good at reading it. I favor *articulating possibilities which bundled determine the degree of their possibility in repetition.*

The uncertainty intrinsic to the future must itself be articulated, and thus far articulation has been at the very center of the analysis. The interrogation of the propositions and hypotheses that are introduced and reformulated is in itself an unpacking of uncertainties that are then rendered discrete. Our initial proposition (Acme Company will employ its industrial sewing machines to assemble the fabrics of YIP shirts and VIP dresses) remains fruitful—that is, rife with potential to render the future, both in terms of opportunities and dangers, discrete. The mention of "YIP shirts" and of "VIP dresses" opens up a new avenue of consideration. What is Acme's capacity for moving, whether rapidly or gradually, from "YIP" textiles to some other source? The delineation of these other sources and the articulation of the rationale for choosing "YIP" over the other suppliers create a semi-calculable opening toward possibility. That is, as these suppliers themselves adapt to changing circumstances, all manner of variables come into play that could not have been predicted. And the key to successful analysis is not to make Jeane Dixon-style predictions. It is to gather and render precise the interplay of elements that with high and low degrees of certainty can be realized. Prediction is a high-stakes game when it addresses a unique individual (person, thing, organization). However, *bundled prediction*, predictions that have bundled sufficient individual propositions together so that something very like margins of sampling error are produced, generates a semi-calculable posture toward the future, toward opportunities and hazards, on the basis of which the degree of sustainable agility and much else can also be specified.

Consider the situation of McDonald's in the late 1940s, when the McDonald brothers decided that *they were in the wrong business*. The automobile was more pervasive than ever before. The price of an automobile ($575 in 1912, $290 in 1927) declined as the guiding concept of the automobile, its purpose, changed radically. The Model T was introduced as "a farmer's car" and, given the state of American roads, this seemed warranted. However, in 1920, for the first time, more American citizens were urban than rural, and there were signs everywhere that the long Jeffersonian dream was over. Congress saw the signs. In 1916 it passed the Federal Aid Road Act, in 1921 the Federal Highway Act.

Ford had fallen asleep at the wheel. Model T owners began in massive numbers to trade in their cars for more stylish ones, and a new market opened up for dealers in used cars. Rather than buy the technologically obsolete Model T for the sake of utility, a used car would serve the purpose—and better. In other words, the automobile was no longer a work horse. It had entered into the world of semiotics, where the consumer becomes what he or she buys, where he or she expresses who he or she is in the thing bought. As such, questions of *style* have to be factored in with those of cost. This was especially the case with the adoption in the automobile industry of installment selling. Competition was centered upon the extremely affordable Model T and credit enabled customers to afford other makes if so inclined. By 1925, 75% of new cars were purchased on installment.

A number of propositions came into play in the first half of this century. An infrastructure was in place for the continued expansion of automobile sales. Institutions and habits of installment buying were locked in. The automobile had been absorbed into the semiotics of what it means to be an American. Utility was in fierce competition with style in automobile purchasing decisions. Alfred Sloan of GM pioneered planned obsolescence in the years prior to the Great Depression and oversaw the company as it displaced Ford from its longstanding market dominance in 1936. Only GM continued to make an annual profit throughout the Great Depression. GM capitalized upon utility and style, on the trends that were already in place by

1929. With a return to prosperity, GM was ideally positioned to make the most of it. The people who had held onto their cars as wages collapsed and unemployment skyrocketed would be standing in line at the war's end to buy a new automobile. Sloan took all of the pertinent propositions and bundled them. In their dialectical-holistic interplay they produced a level of reliability about the future that was actionable, and Ford wouldn't catch up to GM for 50 years.

Ford's *raison d'etre* in affordable utility to the exclusion of convenience and style ("You can have any color as long as it is black") seemed an eternal truth. After all, farmers don't mind that barns tend to be uniformly red. But any illusion about America as a nation of farmers should have been dispelled by 1920. Indeed, there were no indications that America was about to revert to agrarian ways. Bundled predictions pointed in only one direction: the automobile becoming increasingly central to American life. But Ford wasn't bundling his predictions. He was locked into an antiquated model of American life as it relates to the car, and the future he anticipated was the barest extrapolation from these misconceptions.

We have of course moved very rapidly from the seemingly self-evident (Acme company wishes to make a profit in a textile endeavor) into an arena of enormous complexity, of the consideration of entire networks of systems both in the present and the future. But the elegance of our model has not been lost. Our approach to the analysis, whatever the intricacy of the subject matter, remains simple. We have not taken one step from the propositions and hypotheses that we ourselves have stipulated. These propositions and hypotheses insure the rigor of the analysis by serving as a methodological handrail of sorts, an unfailing guide through the most bewildering profusion of phenomena. They are Ariadne's thread through the most daunting labyrinths imaginable.

As the data stream that enters our model for rational consideration swells, there arise organizational considerations. This exigency is reflected in the emergence and formulation of new propositions. An individual person can only cope in his or her decision-making capabilities with a certain amount of information before decision making becomes inefficient and otherwise flawed. As such, it will be necessary to institute areas of specialization within the gathering, movement, and processing of data. And the decision-making and decision-analysis procedure Acme institutes must not only permit this sort of collaboration. It must turn the necessity of collaboration into a positive advantage.

Let's imagine that Acme in fact makes the decision to go with the suppliers YIP and VIP. The decision, irrespective of who has made it, remains securely grounded within a fully articulated matrix of propositions and hypotheses (e.g. Acme Company, by employing its industrial sewing machines to assemble the fabrics of YIP shirts and VIP dresses, will compete successfully with all extant or anticipated competitors). This decision must now enter into a diachronic phase of consideration. That is, it must remain revisable going forward, in light of new realities and fresh opportunities. There must be ongoing *decision analysis*, which is invariably decision reanalysis. Our propositions and hypotheses constitute an analytic point of stability in the organization and comprehension of even the most unstable and evanescent of phenomena (e.g. a mood, a fashion, a buzz, a news cycle, a crisis, a 2007-style Great Recession, a declaration of bankruptcy in the EU).

In the case of Acme, as we have already postulated, it is easy to imagine the kinds of changes that can overtake YIP, VIP, and its competitors, extant and potential. Let's say that median wages in the US continue their steady decline and that a new and more explosive Occupy Wall Street movement arises. Let's posit further that YIP and VIP come within the crosshairs of the Occupy movement for keeping its workers at the lowest levels of remuneration in the industry. The decision has to be made whether to further instantiate the commitments spelled out in Acme's guiding propositions and hypotheses. This could well be a moment for maximizing the benefits of area specialization and collaboration.

We will suppose that Acme has a share with other industry organizations in K-Street representation. This share is under the direct management of a single individual at Acme, Carter Smith. It is Carter's job to mobilize pertinent interests within the industry to further Acme objectives, and toward this end he has founded and vigorously promoted the Textile Roundtable Group, which includes the key K-Street stakeholders and meets regularly to renegotiate a common agenda. Carter decides to call for a meeting of the Group and, in preparation for it, outlines the kind of appeal for action he will make.

We are now indeed within the realm of intangible variables. The repeal of the decision to continue to use YIP and VIP as suppliers cannot be made until a number of other propositions has been addressed. Carter must have the influence to persuade his fellow Group members to act, whether or not they perceive initially the proposed action as in their own best interest. The Textile Roundtable Group must have adequate representation on K Street in order for the agenda that ultimately garners its support to be actionable. But given the enormous uncertainties, the tremendous range of inherently elusive factors that enter into any possible outcome—factors political, economic, psychological, sociological—how do we achieve a bundled prediction that will serve our decision-analysis objective, to determine the viability of Acme's relationship to YIP and VIP?

Acme needs to take up the greatest number of formative elements within the most efficient mode of sampling, and it is fortunate that, to a very great extent, the footwork has already been done. Numerous survey conductors, from Gallup to Zogby International, are already taking the political pulse of the nation and producing numbers complete with delineated margins for sampling error. In addition, software and services for mining the Internet have proliferated like feral kittens in the last several years (e.g. BIRT Analytics, IBM DB2 Intelligent Miner, Oracle Data Mining and so on). The data mining algorithms that go into any measurement of validity have been refined to a very high standard, but our method for rational analysis needn't rely upon purely external assessments. Our method permits the bundling by which any given measurement can be significantly improved with respect to the reduction of uncertainty. As such, Acme not only collects the findings of the most reliable conductors of surveys. It employs data mining to bolster the various sets of survey data. It bundles this information and hence drives down sampling error across the board.

The dialectical interaction of propositions that are bundled lends reliability to a specific course of action. The repetition of the proposition (systematic redundancy) both renders the future discrete, available in the form of opportunity, and creates the openness requisite for agility. This is the betwixt and between of our model. In relation to each other, propositions take on depth. By way of retention and repetition, purblind routinization is obviated and receptivity to novelty maximized.

A holistic model is dialectical, and it is this attribute that makes it time-sensitive. The analytic model is founded fundamentally on the law of noncontradiction ($A = A$). However, over time nothing remains itself. The law promises that everything can be assembled from A's (atoms) and then, for purposes of analysis, be reduced back down to fundamental constitutive elements, and if what is at issue is a mechanical clock, it is quite correct. However, just as physics has moved on from this atomic notion, the rest of us must likewise. We need a model that provides both for elements and relationships that are enduring and those that are fleeting, for stasis (always relative) and flux, and only a dialectical, holistic model can do this. A classic illustration will bear this out.

Richard and Maurice McDonald in 1937 acted on the proposition that a carhop drive-in restaurant east of Pasadena, CA, would turn a profit. This was their A=A moment. Drive-in restaurant equals profitable enterprise. However, without a holistic perspective, the proposition is utterly meaningless. That is, a model has to deal not strictly in static equalities but in change. The proposition in 1937 was indeed a good one. Fifty years before or after, the same proposition would have been, respectively, unintelligible or laughable. The drive-in was a direct function of the popularity of the automobile in the United States, and this popularity was a product of assembly-line mass-manufacturing techniques. Ford gave us one and then the other. If the automobile began as a toy for the wealthy, grounded in the proposition that "The manufacture of automobiles will create a return in light of the numbers of interested wealthy potential customers," it was a proposition that soon had to be changed radically. So A (the manufacture of [necessarily expensive] automobiles to the wealthy) equals A (a profitable undertaking) was no static self-evident truth. The proposition was static, but the truth quickly outpaced it.

What is crucial is the manner of holding the proposition open. Only in this way can it remain agile while deepening in its applicability. At the moment, in 1937, the proposition is a reliable one. However, a number of crucial factors can be determined that account for this, many of them quite intangible. Consider, for instance, the popularity of the automobile. This is obviously a crucial factor with respect to a drive-in restaurant. But what must be observed in this case, that of McDonald's in 1937, is the *nature* of the popularity. The nature of the popularity of the automobile has changed dramatically over the decades. The automobile in 1937 was still associated with geographically and socio-economically prohibited pleasures, with enjoyments that had very recently been impossible. Americans today are still in love with their cars, but massive numbers of them complain about too much time spent in them. The popularity endures, but it is of an entirely different nature.

A constellation of events came together to make McDonald's possible, and by no means was this McDonald's (A) the McDonald's of today (A). California was an especially propitious place for dependence on the automobile. The first carhop drive-in appeared in 1932, the Pig Stand on the corner of Sunset and Vermont, Hollywood. Carpenter's then opened in Los Angeles. Herbert's followed. When McDonald's opened in 1937, it was by no means obvious that it would become a national and then international phenomenon, rather than the others.

The great danger of static thinking (analytic, A=A) is that if Herbert's had done its long-term planning in the 1930s by way of extrapolation from a fixed point (some A=A), it would never have become multibillion-dollar success it became. Wait a minute! Herbert's didn't! Sydney Hoedemaker was an established restaurateur who had very definite ideas grounded in experience about how to make his businesses work. And his entry into the carhop drive-in arena supplied the other operators with much needed credibility, for they were largely mavericks committed to very few received truths.

What it took a maverick to see was that the metabolism of America was changing. While the family meal as a protracted feast persisted in parts of the country, this wasn't the case in California. The new restaurateurs soon discovered that Americans wanted their food cheap and fast, and they didn't at all mind eating in their cars. As such, the walking carhop gave way to the one on roller skates, and then to speaker phones. If the food was cheap, more people could afford to buy it at a time when "eating out" was still considered a luxury. The crucial question of "Why McDonald's?" hasn't yet been answered, but we have come to see how success in the relatively slow paced 1930s was nothing like the outcome of extrapolation on the basis of static models but instead a holistic thinking that could take in the whole changing landscape, a way of forecasting that would actually work without reliance upon a static past (the *causa mortis* for Herbert's). Herbert's operated on a proposition that was not held properly in abeyance, one that was not deepened in its agility by remaining open. This ability to hold a proposition open is as crucial as the content of the proposition itself.

The first McDonald's was a very modest affair. Dick and his brother cooked the hotdogs, made shakes, and served customers on a dozen stools, while three carhops waited on cars in the lot. The eatery did well enough for the brothers to occupy rather grander facilities (600 square feet of interior space) fifty miles east of Los Angeles in San Bernardino, and it was from this location that the McDonalds would earn their fame. San Bernardino was on the verge of becoming a working class boomtown, and the brothers were about to ride a demographic wave the like of which had never been seen before. The unprecedented manufacture of munitions in World War II would bring the Great Depression to an end and usher in a period of economic prosperity so widespread it would come to be known as the Great Prosperity (1947-1975). The proposition with which the brothers had begun contained more potential than even they knew. All they knew was that it was gaining in strength rather than losing it. The widespread growth in income, affecting all classes of society, meant that working class people could now plausibly consider dining out, an experience that was still associated with extravagance. As the restaurants built down (in architecture, menu, kind of service), becoming "joints" as it were, the demographics were changing to create huge numbers of new customers and, as Raymond Ku mentioned, many of these were young people.

By 1948, the McDonalds were wealthy men. Annual profits were in excess of $50,000. They owned the mansion on the hill, quite literally. They bought new Cadillacs every year. What finished the McDonald brothers, at least in terms of their direct role in the business, was the loss of purpose. According to Dick McDonald, "We just became bored." And in the hierarchy of propositions, the loss of motivation or purpose ranks very high.

But there was something else working against the brothers. The imitators they had spawned in San Bernardino were cutting into their customer base, teenagers. For the McDonalds to have continued to grow their restaurant, they would have needed the desire they lacked and the ability to assimilate another proposition:

American families were driven off by the throng of high-school patrons. The carhop drive-in was becoming exclusively associated with the new adolescent culture and it wouldn't have even occurred to many parents to take their kids to one.

By 1948, all manner of data existed to point the way to growth potential, even had the McDonald brothers remained in San Bernardino. The GI Bill was putting more Americans into college than ever before. Munitions makers were benefitting from enormous government contracts in the early days of the Cold War, particularly in the Southwest. The rising median incomes of not just the middle class but of all classes were already evident in the youth culture, an American first made possible by families with so much disposable income that even the kids were making it.

Static adages like "Quality always finds a market" were irrelevant. Quality is relative and in the eye of the beholder. The trick when it comes to branding is the creation of value that is not an intrinsic property of the product (like its weight or mass). When one drinks a Coca-Cola, one drinks more than soda. Coke, as it is said, is iconic, and drinks *this status*. If the truth be known, there isn't an American alive who knows what Coke tastes like in the absence of all the longstanding associated ideas of branding. The truth? In this case, there is none. But the fact is that Coke was invented by a medical doctor in the treatment of nervous disorders and in the promotion of other imagined health benefits. It was in fact medicine.

The professional and the private cannot be neatly separated, and a model that would serve good decision making has personal and business applications. The decision that took the McDonalds out of the fast-food business was a personal one. They got bored. They lost their purpose. The decision that Henry Ford didn't make that took him out of the lead in auto manufacturing was to subject his assumptions, his ruling propositions, to interrogation.

My friend Raymond Ku, former CEO of McDonald's-Taiwan, reflecting back on his years at the company in charge of its Asian operations, told me that a single factor accounts finally for the unprecedented success of this most familiar of institutions: consistency. Raymond had translated every detail of the McDonald's experience into Chinese, a more difficult act of translation being hard to imagine, and he succeeded, and in his success took away the wholly paradoxical idea that the right change was only possible on the basis of what stayed the same throughout, that opportunity could be realized only given the kind of consistency that remains open, even on a moment-to-moment basis, to innovation.

Recently, on my radio program, I addressed the 21st-century business climate in the US and elsewhere with Fran Hawthorne of *Fortune* magazine. This conversation seems a suitable note upon which to conclude our discussion in this book.

McCarty: I am particularly fascinated with the chapter on Starbucks in your book *Ethical Chic*. You set out to find companies that are at once cool and socially responsible, and one you chose was Starbucks. Is your sense that CEO Howard Schultz is for real? Or is he just selling this image of a responsible posture?

Fran Hawthorne: He is more for real than most CEOs, which I confess is a low bar. He is for real about taking care of his workers, in his terms. His father was injured on the job as a truck driver, had no health insurance, and never got back to work. The family was incredible poor. This has stuck with him. Even when Starbucks was doing badly during the 2007 Recession and Wall Street was screaming that he couldn't afford things like healthcare for workers, he kept it. Providing healthcare and stock options, even for part-timers—that aspect is real. It is also real that he fights unions in nasty ways. He has been cited by the National Labor Relations Board for violations. When it comes to the environment, I think Starbucks is overrated. They are not nearly as green as they pretend to be.

McCarty: Schultz gathered data on how much social interaction was taking place in his stores. The inspiration for Starbucks had been a trip he had taken to Italy sometime in the 1980s. He decided that coffee had lost its romance. He thought he could create a place that would induce community. But I think his own research revealed that something like only 10% of patrons actually spoke or interacted with someone other than the barista. He then took out the chair-table combinations and replaced them with long communal tables. But then, of course, people just occupied every other seat.

Hawthorne: I went to more than three dozen Starbucks outlets from Massachusetts to California and sat down near the counter for 15 or 30 minutes and watched. Supposedly the baristas know the customers, but I only saw two cases of this. I saw only eight cases in which the barista and customer chitchatted in some way. This is out of more than 420 interactions. The baristas are talking to each other. The customers are on their iPods or phones. The customers in the store are either on the laptop, reading a physical book or talking with the people they came with. I would see the long tables—which in my local Starbucks have been removed because they didn't work—and, sure enough, people made certain of an empty seat between themselves and the next person. And if that wasn't an option, they went to an individual table. Starbucks is also selling products that are to be consumed at home. So how does this cohere with their self-conception as "the third place," not the office or the home? We are going to be "the front porch." If you are suddenly advertising and pushing take-home instant coffee, you are clearly not expecting interaction.

McCarty: I am not a fan of Starbucks. To me it all sounds like a con. We are this post-modern "third place" and your old-fashioned "front porch." And then there is all of that fake Italian, that gobbledygook they try to make you speak at the counter.

Hawthorne: That's part of their pretentiousness. People who speak Italian just laugh. Of course the words are made up or used improperly.

McCarty: It doesn't seem like it would involve all that much extra effort to get it right.

Hawthorne: I suspect that now that Starbucks has moved into India and China, just everywhere, they are being more careful.

McCarty: McDonald's and Dunkin' Donuts are following the Starbucks lead. McDonald's is taking over the colors and Dunkin' Donuts the Italian names. Are they catching up?

Hawthorne: They are going for a different market, a lower-priced one. During the recession they did much better than they had been. But they are after a different demographic and shifting a bit upscale.

McCarty: How does Starbucks treat the growers, the people who actually produce the coffee for them?

Hawthorne: Starbucks has a certain percentage of fair trade coffee, which must be grown in sustainable ways with farmers receiving a reasonable price. But their coffee is not all fair trade by any means. Some years ago, and there is no doubt about this, Starbucks tried to cheat the farmers of Ethiopia. Two parts of Ethiopia are known in particular for their premium coffee. The government of Ethiopia was trying to get international recognition, trademark the name so that the country itself could make some money by selling the coffee. Europe had agreed to cooperate. But Starbucks had already claimed one of the names Ethiopia wanted to trademark and the company wasn't about to give in. You would think a socially conscious company would be smart enough to know that you don't create a positive public image in the effort to deprive an impoverished country of money. It took Starbucks an amazingly long time to give in on this trademark issue.

McCarty: You know about Walmart and outsourcing to Bangladesh and the horrendous working conditions in that country. Walmart claims that it didn't know where its products were being assembled. How plausible is that?

Hawthorne: Unfortunately, it is very plausible. These supply chains are very long. But the thing is that Walmart could know if it wanted to, and it perhaps doesn't want to.

McCarty: Plausible deniability?

Hawthorne: Yes. I must say, getting back to Starbucks, that I think they provide a great service to society. You can walk into a Starbucks and use the bathroom, maybe it will be clean and maybe not. But you don't have to buy anything, and you can sit there for hours. And this is a public service. This is a service government should be providing, of course. But if it doesn't, I give Starbucks credit for that.

McCarty: In the mid-1990s, however, Starbucks found themselves in quite a mess with respect to child labor. Children were being used in Guatemala to grow Starbucks coffee. Starbucks claimed ignorance and that they had no way of knowing who was growing their coffee—shades of Walmart in Bangladesh here.

Hawthorne: Companies that get caught using child labor or abused labor can pay a big price. Companies want an ethical image.

McCarty: The public knew that Nike had sweatshops all over Southeast Asia. What kind of price did Nike pay for that?

Hawthorne: They paid a price. They had a terrible public image and it is still with them. Students insisted that their colleges not use Nike.

****

In a world run by criminal syndicates and multinational corporations, will the profit motive ever coincide with ethical behavior? Fran Hawthorne is more optimistic than I am. In my view, our thinking has to change dramatically if we are going to live properly, a notion which includes the ethical conduct of business. It seems to me that the emphasis on consumers solving the problem—by recycling, by attending to ethical companies, to educating themselves, buying a hybrid vehicle—represents a massive displacement. No matter how many jars of Prego you fish from the garbage, you will make no dent in the damage a Dow Chemical does in an hour. Blaming the consumer, making him or her feel responsible, is an ideological ruse that serves those who are truly culpable. It keeps us all distracted—as do TVs and video games—while the real damage is done in Washington, D.C., and Beijing and Moscow.

The analytic, nature-mastering, mathematical reasoning that Raymond Ku found so impressive in the brief history of America seems to be a dead end. The case in this regard is complex, but I can offer a hint of it in these terms: For as long as the ballistic missile comes in advance of the anti-ballistic missile, for as long as there is a window separating a technology of destruction from defense against that technology, global catastrophe is a mathematical certainty. Technological advance is accelerating. The destruction of the world is much more than merely possible. We can destroy it and, I think, given enough time, we will. Unless we recognize another way of thinking, the dialectical-holistic style I have tried to set forth in this book, we will not only be rather stupid, rather wrong rather often, we will soon be quite dead.